Dear Israelis, Dear Arabs

Books by Roger Fisher

INTERNATIONAL CONFLICT FOR BEGINNERS

DEAR ISRAELIS, DEAR ARABS

Dear Israelis, Dear Arabs

A Working Approach to Peace

Roger Fisher

1817

HARPER & ROW, PUBLISHERS
New York, Evanston, San Francisco, London

FIRST EDITION

STANDARD BOOK NUMBER: 06-011274-3

LIBRARY OF CONGRESS CATALOG CARD NUMBER: 74-181618

Designed by C. Linda Dingler

Arab-Israeli Conflict

Contents

Foreword

This is an unusual book. To say that it is "unique" would be to imply an omniscient familiarity with past publications that I do not claim to possess. Suffice it to say that I doubt if there is anything quite like it. How to describe it? The book presumes to be a sort of marriage counsellor to two unmarried, and indeed antagonistic states, telling each one in turn what mistakes to avoid and what affirmative courses may be productive of good and in the state's self-interest; even to supply them both with drafts of letters they should write to each other or to third parties who have a role to play; to be frankly and unashamedly and quite openly an inter-mediator and to tell the world about it with all modesty but in the hope of stimulating others to make better proposals if they can. This is no secret negotiation now revealed in what might be called the "Roger Fisher Papers"; this is open correspondence, openly arrived at.

Roger Fisher, Professor of Law at the Harvard Law School, has been a United States official, a practicing attorney, an adviser to governments—at one point simultaneously a consultant in inter-national affairs for the Government of the United States and a registered foreign agent seeking a solution for the microproblems of the microstatic island of Anguilla. In the Middle East he has explored the possibilities of peace between the Arabs and Israel as a consultant-member of a Quaker group; in other capacities he has conversed with Nasser, Hussein and Golda Meir and leaders in the Palestinian camp. His last trip, on his own, was in July, 1971.

He has written and collected in this volume letters to anonymous (but real) Egyptian, Israeli, Palestinian, Jordanian, American and United Nations officials.

Roger Fisher notes that it "is comparatively easy to come up with suggestions of things that ought to happen," like making the streets of New York clean and safe. But these letters are different; they "suggest some of the things that some of the parties could do. Collectively they propose an approach to the problem. But they do not purport to provide a comprehensive solution. . . . I was not trying to play God," he says. He points out to his friends in all these quarters what moves, actually made or contemplated, are counterproductive and persuasively suggests if his correspondent would write a letter or issue a statement in the following terms (which are then drafted verbatim), such and such advantages might be expected to follow. He uses in part a technique which has been tried elsewhere: put yourself in the other fellow's shoes and think out why he feels as he does about you. He has practiced that preachment so much himself you feel he must almost be a centipede!

To the surprise of some of his correspondents, he remains totally uncommitted and nonpartisan. His wise and shrewd advice can be acted on by the persons concerned partly because he never attempts a package solution for the entire problem of the future relations of Arabs and Israelis in the Middle East. It is not a shotgun approach since he is a political sharpshooter who selects as targets a series of individual detailed troubles which he proceeds to eliminate, such as suggesting that Egypt invite Air France to negotiate daily flights between Cairo and Tel Aviv and that tourist exchanges be facilitated from both sides.

No one interested in the Middle East—or in the process of coping with an international conflict—should ignore this book. If any approach can lessen the Arab-Israeli stalemate, Roger Fisher's approach may be it. He demonstrates persuasively that the critical task is not to talk *about* a conflict, but to deal with it—not to debate past mistakes or distant goals, but to suggest specific next steps.

He ends with a "Note to the Reader" which challenges the

reader to *do* something about the Middle East mess by identifying "some individual or organization" as a "target of influence" and by formulating and communicating to the "target" practical proposals for action. He then dares to include a few blank pages so that the reader can begin to put his thoughts down on paper before he puts down the book. As I said at the outset, this is an unusual book.

PHILIP C. JESSUP

Acknowledgments

It is impossible to thank all those who have contributed to the development of these ideas and these drafts. Mention must, however, be made of Professor Gidon Gottlieb and George Frampton, Jr. Professor Gottlieb has for several years been developing concepts that could contribute to a peaceful settlement in the Middle East. I have drawn on his work and his thinking, particularly his idea of a common state of Palestine and his suggestion of sample withdrawal. I hope that his elaboration of those and other concepts for a peaceful settlement will be published soon.

George Frampton, Jr., is a close friend who worked with me full time for several months on the Middle East as he has on other matters. He wrote some of the drafts included in the letters, and earlier versions of others. I only regret that commitments elsewhere prevented his working with me on the letters themselves. Although not responsible for the words, he is a true coauthor of many of the ideas.

Some of the drafts were originally prepared for discussion by the working party of the International Quaker Middle East Peace Research Project as part of an effort to identify on the operational level diverse approaches to reaching a just and lasting peace in the Middle East. These drafts, for which I was responsible, were privately discussed with individuals in the Middle East and elsewhere as a means of promoting the examination of a variety of peacemaking concepts. At no time were they proposals for which approval or agreement was sought from any individual or group.

They have never been endorsed by any government official or political faction or by any Quaker group or organization.

In all discussions and in writing these letters I have acted as a private citizen on my own responsibility. They reflect that guideline of private diplomacy: "Sometimes speak to a government official; never speak for one."

Dear Israelis, Dear Arabs

Introduction

There is a great difference between discussing facts and dealing with them. This book tries to deal actively with the facts of the Arab-Israeli conflict. The bulk of the book consists of letters written during the summer of 1971 to individual officials in Jerusalem, Cairo, and elsewhere with whom I have discussed the Arab-Israeli conflict and who are involved in it. The letters have been edited to omit some names, to improve clarity, and to avoid excess length and duplication. Within the letters are drafts of operational documents, illustrating in specific terms how particular ideas might be put into action. The letters are preceded by a general memorandum of advice, a copy of which was sent with each of the individual letters. Each addressee was told that I was writing comparable letters to others involved in the Arab-Israeli conflict and that he would receive copies of those letters.

As I think about it, I had four purposes in writing these letters. The first purpose was to convey my ideas to the individuals to whom the letters were addressed. Each of those to whom I wrote had given generously of his time. Each had expressed an interest in my general approach. Some had explicitly asked me to write and to apply that approach to the problems with which they were faced. All had indicated that suggestions would be welcome. First of all, then, the letters are a straightforward response to those expressions of interest.

Second, the letters constituted a kind of research project for myself. I have long been convinced that the cutting edge of theory lies in its application to fact. Much of the merit of Machiavelli's *Prince* comes from the fact that he was not just writing about foreign affairs, he was trying to advise a prince as to what he ought to do. Could Machiavelli have given equally persuasive advice to the prince's adversaries? Having tried to advise them, might he have been able to produce still better advice to the prince? To the extent that political science is a science, one ought to be able to give constructive advice to each player in the international political contest.

A few years ago I worked with a freshman seminar writing a *Handbook for Demonstrators* that included a last chapter called "How to Frustrate a Demonstration." We concluded that by withholding our judgment on the merits of a controversy we could better understand the structure of the conflict and better devise strategies enabling each party to pursue his interests with less unnecessary conflict. I wanted similarly to learn more about the nature of international conflict through trying to write letters of advice to adversaries, giving each of them some ideas on how they might best pursue their own enlightened self-interest. Just as in a football contest between teams with different strengths, or in a sailing race between different kinds of boats, the best advice for one party will not be identical with that for another.

A third purpose looked to my students and academic colleagues as an audience. Too often we teachers serve as a model not of problem-solving but of writing about problems. Learning should not simply be a pleasure in itself; it should contribute to the solution of public problems. I have already used these letters in a seminar trying to teach law students the skills of coping with conflict. The letters have also served to stimulate discussion about the purposes of scholarship and about the dangers of becoming too deeply involved on the one hand and too little involved on the other.

Finally, as I wrote the letters I began to contemplate their publication as a means of generating discussion among a wider group on alternative ways of dealing with international conflict in general and with the Arab-Israeli conflict in particular. In the Middle East, as in many other conflict situations, confrontation tends to lead to stalemate. Government officials on all sides see themselves as having few options. They feel confined by public opinion, which appears to allow little room for flexibility. Each member of the public, in turn, often feels that he is helplessly confined at the hands of the officials. Public discussion of a substantial number of different steps that might be taken could serve to open up the debate, relieve the sense of stalemate, and provide more latitude for movement.

A reader of the letters will want to know something more about the writer, his relationship to the Middle East, and what he is trying to do. Let me attempt an explanation.

For the past thirty years the process of coping with conflict has had a continuing interest for me—as an undergraduate major in international law and relations, as a participant in World War II, as a United States government official in Paris during the years of the Marshall Plan, as a Washington lawyer practicing international law, as an adviser to more than one foreign government, as an advocate arguing cases in court, as a consultant on international security affairs to the Department of Defense, and as a professor of law. Some friends are confused by the fact that I am an active board member of both the peace-concerned Council for a Livable World and Herman Kahn's Hudson Institute, and that I was simultaneously both a consultant for the United States and a registered foreign agent (for the runaway Caribbean island of Anguilla). The focus of my interest throughout this time has been on process: How does one best carry on a conflict so as to advance the interests in which he or she is legitimately interested without causing needless violence? That concern has been reflected in the titles of things I have written such as: "Fractionating Conflict,"[1] "Do We Want to Win the Cold War?,"[2] "Bringing Law to Bear on Governments,"[3] "International Relations Theory for the Decision-Maker,"[4] and *International Conflict for Beginners,*[5] published in London under the title *Basic Negotiating Strategy.*[6] The central focus of my research and teaching is on roles for law in conflict resolution. I am trying to develop some theory (by which I mean some useful distinctions and some plausible hypotheses) derived from practice and to apply that theory to practice.

It is that background, rather than a deep study of the geography and peoples of the Middle East, that I bring to the Arab-Israeli conflict. Following visits to the area in 1954 and 1966, I had the unusual opportunity in May 1970 to meet President Nasser of Egypt, King Hussein of Jordan, and Prime Minister Meir of Israel in connection with television interviews for the public television series *The Advocates*. The substantive discussions I then had, particularly with President Nasser, and the discussions with others to which those interviews led, convinced me that there was at least a small chance that the situation might be improved.

During the course of 1970 and 1971 I made three additional trips to the Middle East, visiting Amman, Beirut, Cairo, and Jerusalem. On two of these trips I traveled under Quaker auspices as a consultant member of a group exploring the prospects for peace. The final visit that preceded the writing of these letters, a trip I took in July 1971 to Jerusalem and Cairo, was under no one's auspices but my own.

So much for me and my involvement. Those who have read the letters indicate that more of an explanation is needed as to their approach and their purpose. The letters are said to be inconsistent and incomplete. It has also been said that even if Israel, Egypt, Jordan, and the Palestinians were to follow the advice that is proffered there would still be no complete peace in the Middle East. And what about the Russians and the Chinese?

Each letter is written to *its* audience. It is an attempt to convey constructive suggestions as to what that party might do to pursue its enlightened self-interest. Each party has an interest not only in victory but also in peace. What I have tried to do is to suggest some specific, operational steps that in my judgment each party might reasonably consider taking within the next six months or so. Each suggestion requires not only a balance between that party's interest in victory and its interest in peace, but also a balance between what is desirable and what is acceptable. In writing each party my major purpose is not to say that a particular substantive suggestion is *the* answer. My purpose is rather to suggest and in fact to argue for an approach to the situation. By making particular suggestions I am saying that there are many things—like these— that the parties should be considering and doing.

It is comparatively easy to come up with suggestions of things that ought to happen: The United Nations ought to become more effective; our economic resources should be more wisely allocated; the Vietnam War should be brought to an end; unnecessary delays in the judicial system should be eliminated; the streets of New York City should be made clean and safe; and so forth. It is more difficult to come up with specific suggestions as to who should do what tomorrow morning. Improving the Arab-Israeli conflict, like improving New York City, is going to require specific and concurrent efforts by a large number of people over a period of years.

These letters suggest some things that some of the parties could do. Collectively they propose an approach to the problem. But they do not purport to provide a comprehensive solution.

First, I have not given advice to everybody. There is no letter to a Russian, nor are there letters to friends in Britain, France, Lebanon, Syria, or Saudi Arabia, to name other states that could substantially affect, for better or worse, the Arab-Israeli conflict. The Soviet role, in particular, is likely to be important if not crucial. As one Egyptian put it to me, "We are risking some of our independence in order to get back our territory." It is a dangerous game. One can only hope that the Soviet Union fully appreciates the degree to which its interests are advanced through international order and peace as well as through "victories." I do not believe that I have enough "feel" for the Soviet position to write a letter that might be regarded by a Soviet official as embodying their enlightened self-interest. A general strategy for limiting the Soviet military role in the Middle East includes, in my view, measures promoting peace that would reduce the Egyptian interest in a Soviet presence. From my vantage point the Soviet Union is part of the problem, not part of the answer.

The absence of a hypothetical Soviet letter, like the absence of other letters that might have been written, is irrelevant to the merits of the letters that are here. Each letter contains advice that is submitted as being worthy of consideration whether or not any other party follows the advice that is given them. Each letter stands on its own merits, not as part of a master plan. Each letter is independent of the others. I was not trying to play God.

Second, the advice attempts to be realistic, not utopian. Rather than discussing a final solution it deals with next steps. If the suggestions advanced were adopted there would still be conflict, but it would be carried on in a more civilized and constructive way. Face-to-face discussions would be taking place, Israeli citizens would be visiting Cairo, Palestinian refugees would be returning to the West Bank, and limited withdrawal of Israeli forces would have taken place. To advance proposals that go much further seems unduly optimistic.

Each letter should be judged in terms of its addressee. If, for example, you were addressing a member of the executive committee of the Palestine Liberation Organization, and wanted there to be at least some chance of his following your advice, what else would you ask him to do? I find that many are unwilling to accept this test of trying to be realistic. Some who believe that there is no chance of persuading Palestinians to be reasonable at all will criticize a letter unless it asks them to be angels.

Finally, there is no attempt here to present a complete and balanced picture of the issues and facts underlying the various aspects of the Arab-Israeli conflict as they might be summarized by a historian. Readers are encouraged to look elsewhere for background information. Here you are looking over the shoulder of some participant as he receives suggestions as to what he might do.

As you read the letters and drafts, mark them up. If ideas occur to you that you think would be better, make a note of them. Pages 151 to 153 are for that purpose. And let somebody hear from you. Who do you think should do what tomorrow? Is there something you can do that would make that action more likely?

1.

General Memorandum

An Approach to the Middle East

[A copy of this memorandum
accompanied each of the letters which follow it.]

Work on What Ought to Happen

Among the millions of words that have been written about the
Arab-Israeli conflict the most significant differences lie not in the
point of view but rather in the question that—implicitly if not explicitly—is being discussed. Some of the questions to which major
attention is directed are the following:

What Happened. A lot of historical research is directed toward
establishing objective facts. Who did what when?

It is difficult to criticize the search for objective historical truth,
but a shortage of historical facts is not a major contributing factor
to the difficulties of the Middle East. We have too many facts, not
too few. Historical facts in themselves have no objective importance. They are important to somebody only for some purpose.
If we know the current question, and who is faced with a choice,
then we can gather data relevant to that person and that choice.

What Caused Past Events to Happen. A second, and more sub-
jective, kind of historical research is the search for causes. What
caused the war of 1948 or the war of 1967? What caused the Security Council to do what it did? And so forth. The search for a
primary cause is fascinating, but what will it tell us? There are a
dozen explanations for every important event—economic consid-
erations, political forces, psychological strains, cultural patterns,
historical trends, personal bias, bad intentions, poor judgment—
and most of them will be true. In hindsight it all depends upon

what is taken as given and what is taken as subject to change. Arguing over the causes of past events is stimulating but unproductive.

Who Was Right and Who Was Wrong. The passing of moral judgment is essential if we are to retain moral values that have a cutting edge—that can affect what we do. But too often debate over the Middle East is intended not to illuminate what ought to be done but rather to persuade us to pass an either/or judgment condemning "the Arabs" or "the Jews." In effect we are asked: Judging between these two shades of gray, don't you agree that this one is white and that one is black?

What Is Legal. Law has a large and constructive role to play in conflict resolution, but no court is going to hand down a legal decision that resolves the Arab-Israeli conflict. It is useful to have governments know that their actions will be subjected to examination by men learned in international law and that scholars will judge the legality of their actions. However, legal criticism is not of primary importance here. If the Arab-Israeli dispute were to be resolved by a court on the basis of law, then preparing persuasive briefs on legal issues would certainly be a constructive task. But if the crucial decisions are those to be made by, say, the governments of Israel, Egypt, the Soviet Union, and the United States, then arguing over the legality of the 1948 Partition of Palestine by the United Nations is of limited use.

Whose Fault Is the Present Situation. Israeli and Arab officials have become so cynical about each other's intentions that they now make little attempt to influence each other. Each step in the diplomatic dance is intended not to lead to a successful partnership but rather to cause the potential partner to stumble in public and thus to convince the spectators that the failure is his fault. The United States is seen as the most important spectator. In every speech, in every newspaper, the debate is carried on as though the most pressing question were that of comparative moral fault. Government officials and journalists throughout the Middle East seek to demonstrate that their government has done all that can reasonably be asked of it, and that it is now the other side's turn to be constructive.

Success, however, is measured by results, not by a tally of merits and demerits for each side. As with a group of quarreling passengers in a lifeboat at sea, some of whom are bailing, some steering, and some handling the sail, the relevant question for each is not, Have I done as much as the others? but rather, Is there anything more I can do which will improve my chances enough to justify the effort? For each of the participants in the Middle East dispute, preoccupation with what others have done is hardly the best tactic for improving the situation. If the Middle East conflict gets worse and worse, no one will be adequately compensated by knowing that history will say others were more to blame than he.

What Are Their Real Intentions. In Israel one is asked the true intentions of the Egyptians. "Do they truly want peace? Or don't the Arabs really want to destroy Israel and drive the Jews from the Middle East?" In Egypt, Jordan, and elsewhere in the Arab world one is asked about the true intentions of the Israelis. "Do they truly want peace? Or don't the Israelis really want to expand into Arab land, drive the Arabs off, and populate the area with all the world's Jews?"

Governments always have mixed intentions. What governments decide to do is the product of circumstances and a concurrence of individual views and forces. Little is to be gained from searching for or criticizing some hypothetical single intention.

What Is Probably Going to Happen. Most of those who look toward the future do so with the spectator's point of view: "I wonder what is going to happen." Predicting what will probably happen about a problem contributes little to its solution. Predicting has in fact an inhibiting quality of tending to convince people that the future is fixed, and that there is nothing we can do about it. If in any sense the future is determined, it is equally determined that we must behave as if we have free will. One cannot get up in the morning wondering what pair of trousers fate has determined that he will wear that day. One has to decide what pair of trousers to wear, just as one must decide what if anything to do about the Middle East.

A Better Question: What Ought to Happen?

Everyone concerned with the Middle East necessarily makes an implicit or explicit judgment about the most useful questions to which he should devote his time and effort. Anyone who spends his time advancing arguments as to why Israel as a Jewish state does not have a right to exist is implicitly asserting that that is the greatest contribution he can make to the present situation. Someone who devotes his time to advancing arguments as to why Israel as a Jewish state *does* have a right to exist is essentially making the same implicit assertion—namely, that debating that question is the greatest contribution he can make. Those who argue about historical facts, from one point of view or another, are equally making the common assertion that such debate is a wise and effective use of their time and talents. Or they are implicitly saying that they do not really care about what happens.

To engage in such debate is to fiddle while Rome burns. It is to argue over navigational mistakes of the past while the ship goes on the rocks.

The most important task in the Middle East is to make it a better place tomorrow than it is today. The greatest need is to figure out some things that people should do to improve the situation, and to make it more likely that they will do them. There will be quarrels enough about what ought to be done and who ought to do it. To devote our attention to these questions is to devote attention to questions that make a difference. Every day decisions are being made either consciously or by default. With more intellectual resources devoted to what ought to happen rather than to the past or to assessments of comparative fault, we might be able to end up in a better place.

Break Up the Problem

The Middle East is not one problem; it is many. There is a natural desire to solve big problems. People ask for *the* solution to *the* problem of crime, to *the* problem of violence, to *the* television problem, or to *the* drug problem. Anyone who works in one of these areas quickly learns that there is no one solution—that in fact there is no one problem.

The Arab-Israeli situation is no different. Many Arabs and many Israelis like to think of the situation as a simple struggle between two sides, between good and evil. Even those in no way involved tend to think of the situation as "a" dispute subject to "a" solution.

The Security Council resolution of November 22, 1967, although interpreted differently by the parties concerned, provides a framework for current efforts to deal with the Arab-Israeli conflict.[7] That resolution refers to "a" settlement. The late President Gamal Abdel Nasser, in accepting the resolution, accepted the idea of "a package deal." He recognized that Egypt should not expect Israel to withdraw—as provided for in the resolution—without Egypt's going forward with respect to other aspects of the resolution, such as assured access for Israel through the Suez Canal and the Gulf of Aqaba, and a formal commitment to live in peace with Israel. Israel also has voiced opposition to partial measures, suggesting that it should not be asked to withdraw any of its military forces from any of the territories occupied in 1967 until a final peace treaty has been negotiated and signed.

How is it most useful to think of the Arab-Israeli situation for the purpose of dealing with it? During the past four years the conventional wisdom as to how a peaceful outcome to Arab-Israeli differences might be brought about has run along the following lines, creating the illusion that there was but one problem:

Negotiations were to take place through Ambassador Gunnar Jarring, the Secretary-General's Special Representative appointed under Security Council Resolution 242 of November 22, 1967. He would start off meeting separately with the two sides and, as progress developed, would arrange for some meetings involving face-to-face discussions, which would culminate in the formal signing of a peace agreement. The peace agreement or treaty would arrange for the settlement, in stages, of all aspects of the problem. Upon the carrying out of the agreement, Resolution 242 would have been implemented and the dispute settled.

Is this a realistic prospect? The answer, unfortunately, must be no. Without prejudging the substance of a comprehensive peace agreement, one can illustrate the many pieces that would be included in such a package deal:

PIECES OF A PACKAGE DEAL

1. An agreement between Egypt and Israel defining the final Sinai boundary.

2. An Israeli-Egyptian agreement defining the extent of demilitarized zones along their boundary, what is not to take place within these zones, what international or other personnel are to supervise compliance with such rules, how disputes about the zones are to be settled, and how and when such arrangements are to be brought into being, maintained, and terminated.

3. If international personnel are to be involved, the agreed text of a Security Council resolution, agreements with the various governments that will provide personnel, covering compensation, and all other related matters.

4. An Israeli-Egyptian agreement covering the rights of Israeli ships and shipping in the Suez Canal.

5. An agreement among the four states on the Gulf of Aqaba (Israel, Jordan, Saudi Arabia, and Egypt) defining the substantive rights of ships and airplanes in and over the Gulf and the procedures for settling disputes and for implementing, maintaining, and revising the rights agreed upon.

6. An agreement with guarantor states or an agreed text of a Security Council resolution making continued compliance with the Gulf of Aqaba agreement more likely.

7. An agreement between Jordan and representatives of the Palestinian people accepting the sovereignty of Jordan over the West Bank and assuring their rights within Jordan.

8. An agreement between Israel and Jordan governing the boundaries of Gaza and establishing and governing the arrangements for freedom of access between Gaza and the West Bank.

9. An agreement between Jordan and Palestinian representatives in Gaza establishing and governing the relationship between Gaza and Jordan.

10. An agreement between Jordan and Israel defining the boundary between them.

11. An agreement between Israel and Jordan defining the extent of demilitarized zones along their boundary, what is not to take place within those zones, what international or other personnel are to supervise compliance with such rules, how disputes about the zones are to be settled, and how and when such arrangements are to be brought into being, maintained, and terminated.

12. An agreement between Israel and Jordan defining the boundaries of Jerusalem, access to Israeli and Arab boroughs within Jerusalem, and international arrangements governing these boroughs. This agreement might include:

   a. A document establishing the political aspects of the Arab borough in Jerusalem, defining the extent of its jurisdiction and the rules and governmental arrangements applicable within it.

   b. A document establishing the political aspects of the Jewish borough in Jerusalem, defining the extent of its jurisdiction and the rules and governmental arrangements applicable within it.

   c. A document establishing the political aspects of the unified city of Jerusalem including both boroughs, defining the rules and governmental arrangements of the city as a whole.

   d. A document defining the boundaries of special holy places within the city of Jerusalem and the rules and other arrangements regarding them, including questions of access, custody, and power to make alterations.

   e. The agreed text of legislation or constitutional arrangements to be adopted by Israel with respect to Jerusalem.

   f. The agreed text of legislation or constitutional arrangements to be adopted by Jordan with respect to Jerusalem.

   g. The agreed text of a General Assembly or Security Council resolution confirming and approving the arrangements with respect to Jerusalem.

13. An agreement between Israel and Jordan governing economic and customs matters, at least with respect to trade with Jerusalem.

14. An agreement between Israel and Syria defining the boundary between them.

15. An agreement between Israel and Syria defining the status of the Golan Heights area, what is not to take place within designated zones, what international or other personnel are to supervise compliance with such rules, how disputes about the zones are to be resolved, and how and when such arrangements are to be brought into being, maintained, and terminated.

16. If international personnel are to be involved in the Golan Heights area, the agreed text of a Security Council resolution, and the agreements with those who will provide the personnel, covering financial and all other matters.

17. An agreement between Israel and Lebanon confirming their boundary and releasing claims with respect to all other matters outstanding between them.

18. Israeli legislation defining the rights of Palestinians who lived in 1948 in what has become Israel and who left in 1948 or thereafter, with respect to returning or not returning to Israel and with respect to compensation; legislation establishing procedures for processing claims.

19. An agreement between Israel and the World Bank establishing an international development fund to be used for new towns, development projects, and loans for Palestinians who for one reason or another do not settle within Israel.

20. An agreement between the World Bank and nations agreeing to contribute to the international development fund for the Palestinians.

21. An agreement between Israel and the leaders of Palestinian organizations accepting the state and boundaries of Israel and the financial and immigration measures undertaken by Israel and renouncing all further claims against Israel beyond those provided in the new arrangements.

22. An agreement among the states of Israel, Lebanon, Syria, and Jordan governing the uses of waters of the Jordan River and its tributaries.

23. An agreement between Egypt and Israel settling the claims of Jews who have moved from Egypt to Israel.

24. An agreement between Syria and Israel settling the claims of Jews who have moved from Syria to Israel.

25. An agreement between Jordan and Israel settling the claims of Jews who have moved from Jordan to Israel.

26. An agreement between Iraq and Israel settling the claims of Jews who have moved from Iraq to Israel.

27. An agreement between Israel and all Arab states participating in the Arab boycott of companies doing business in Israel, formally accepting the existence of Israel, committing these states to live in peace with Israel, and officially ending the boycott.

A comprehensive settlement would include substantially all of those subsidiary agreements and perhaps more besides. Such a complex of parties and provisions is not going to be reached by having any one man, such as Ambassador Jarring, going back and forth between "the two sides," nor even by having "both sides" meet for face-to-face discussions with him. A brief glance at the possible contents of a comprehensive settlement demonstrates, without question, that: there are many different substantive questions; some questions primarily involve some parties, while others primarily involve different parties; and some issues can be decided independently of others, while some can be decided only after others have been resolved.

In short, for purposes of being dealt with peacefully, *the* Arab-Israeli dispute is not a single problem in need of a single settlement. It is a complex of interrelated issues involving diverse substantive questions to be faced by differing groups and individuals at different times.

Work on the Process

Progress toward peace will depend upon the procedures used. With respect to adversaries it is often assumed that "when they are ready to get down to hard bargaining they will do so." Despite the ambiguity and uncertainty in our own views we tend to take an adversary's intentions as fixed. Obviously, the attitudes, values, and goals of those who make up a government are important, but equally important are the occasions for decision on which those states of mind are brought to bear. The answers produced by a government depend upon the questions asked, and procedure is what determines which questions are asked when. Procedure controls the formulation and timing of the choices with which the parties are confronted; for any given mix of attitudes and objectives procedure can have a crucial effect on what happens.

It is generally unwise at a time of distrust and hostility to pursue a procedure that asks an adversary to take a clear position on an ultimate question. When an intermediary asks each side to state publicly its position on an ultimate question, he is likely to induce each side to take an extreme position. Having publicly stated a position, a government finds it more difficult to be flexible in the future. At the outset the publicly stated position may have been thought of as a negotiating position that was padded with plenty of fat. Over time that fat tends to turn to bone. A subsequent position will be judged less on its merits than by the degree to which it departs from the original position.

The governments of the Middle East have already said a great deal about their positions. No procedure should be pursued that will stimulate them to dig themselves further into official positions from which it will be increasingly difficult to extricate them. More generally, attention should be devoted less to arguing about substantive disagreements and more to considering the procedures by which those disagreements are to be dealt with.

Be Operational

The constant effort should be to affect for the better what is going to happen. This means that less attention should be devoted to positions, opinions, criticisms, arguments, views, reactions, and statements of policy, and more attention should be devoted to offers, delegations of authority, proposals, decisions, instructions, and on-the-ground action. Some kinds of governmental statements are like an after-dinner speech or a bull session, like cocktail conversation or social chatter. The words fill a given amount of time. They disclose something about the attitude or thinking of the speaker, but they rarely cause things to happen. An effective business meeting is likely to end up with somebody having written on a yellow pad who is going to do what, and when and where the next meeting is going to take place. The difference between words and operational words is striking. In the Middle East we need more attention to operational words.

Think About Their *Decision*

Although the normal approach for any government is to think first about its own decision—how it should react to what some other government has said or done—the starting point should be the other government's problems. What is the decision that we would like them to make, or to refrain from making? After we have identified some possible decisions we would like them to make, we can then consider what we might do to move events in that direction.

The government of the United States, for example, is properly concerned with the increasing military and political role of the Soviet Union in the Middle East. The normal reaction is to study it, make speeches about it, and to warn others of its seriousness. A better approach would be first to consider what restraints on Soviet behavior might realistically be hoped for. What decisions might the Soviet Union take in the future that would be favored by the United States? A list of theoretical possibilities might include decisions to:

- Refrain from increasing Soviet military personnel in the area
- Remove all Soviet military personnel now stationed in the Middle East
- Refrain from increasing Soviet naval forces in the Mediterranean
- Report publicly all arms deliveries to Egypt and to other Arab states

- Agree to discuss in advance with the United States all proposed arm shipments to the Middle East
- Restrict arms shipments below certain designated limits
- Formally affirm the right of Soviet Jews to emigrate to Israel
- Resume diplomatic relations with Israel
- Enter into a treaty of friendship with Israel

For the United States to start with such a consideration of things it might want the Soviet Union to do or refrain from doing automatically stimulates consideration of things that the United States might do to help matters move in a desired direction. Speeches by officials about the threat of the Soviet presence in the Middle East are not likely to reduce that threat. United States arms shipments to Israel, like Soviet arms shipments to Egypt, are by themselves not likely to cool the situation.

If a government's actions are to be a rational cause of future events rather than a simple consequence of past events, that government should think about the future events that it wants to cause.

2.

Letter to an Egyptian

August 10, 1971

Dear _____ [an official of the government of Egypt],

With the thought that you might be interested in my present views about Egypt's position and what it ought to do, I have tried to set them down in this letter, which is a revised version of a rough draft I left in Cairo on July 9.

Enclosed is a memorandum that sets forth an approach to the Middle East problem. This letter applies that approach to the question of what Egypt ought to do. I am writing similar letters, copies of which I shall send you, to an Israeli friend, to a Palestinian friend, and to others.

General Approach

As indicated in the joint communiqué issued July 4 following the Foreign Minister's discussions in Moscow,[8] the effort remains to pursue "a settlement to the problem through political means based on the implementation of all the provisions of the Security Council Resolution 242." "Through political means" requires exerting influence on the government of Israel that will cause that government to make some decisions.

Israel is unlikely to make decisions acceptable to Egypt unless the political cost of not doing so is increased. High political costs will not result simply from a failure to reach agreement with the

Arabs. Such costs might, however, be anticipated if Israel were repeatedly to reject specific proposals that appear to be fair.

A year ago the predominant question in the United States was, Why don't the Arabs want to make peace? During the past year Egypt accepted Secretary of State Rogers' initiative,[9] accepted the cease-fire,[10] offered to open the Suez Canal prior to total withdrawal,[11] accepted Jarring's February 8 proposal,[12] and welcomed Secretary Rogers to Cairo.[13] Today the question as seen in the United States is quite different: Is Israel justified in dragging its feet? Despite the bad impression of Egypt in the United States caused by the prompt breakdown of the military standstill during the first ninety days of the cease-fire, Israel is now politically on the defensive.

Some Egyptians assert that the Nasser-Sadat strategy of politically isolating Israel by demonstrating the legitimacy and reasonableness of the Arab position has failed, that Egypt cannot afford to make any more "concessions," and that the time has come for a return to a more bellicose approach. But that is surely wrong. If anything failed, it was the old bellicose approach in which Egypt rattled the saber and waited for others to take the political initiative. The political moves that Egypt has made during 1970–71 were not "concessions" in the sense of giving something for nothing. Each involved some domestic political cost, but produced political results in the desired direction. Firing an artillery shell across the Canal also involves domestic costs, financial and otherwise; it produces the unfortunate political result of increased support for Israel. If by sending a piece of paper on its way one can get better results than by sending an artillery shell on its way, then the piece of paper is a weapon, not a "concession."

In seeking to exert influence on Israel, both directly and through the United States, Egypt should do what it can to affect Israeli and American perceptions of the three basic elements:

1. What will happen if Israel fails to make decisions leading to withdrawal

2. What will happen if Israel does make the decisions desired by Egypt

3. What precise decisions are desired by Egypt

1. Strengthening Israeli Awareness of the Adverse Consequences of Not Making Decisions to Withdraw

There are two distinct kinds of warning that Egypt should convey credibly to the Israeli government. One is a warning of the long-term danger to Israel if it fails to make peace and withdraw from Arab territory in the near future. The other is a warning of the short-term consequences to the Israeli government if it fails to make those specific decisions that are proposed as steps toward a peaceful settlement. Neither type of warning can be effectively conveyed by a simple threat or speech. Each could benefit from careful planning.

a. THE LONG-TERM CONSEQUENCES FOR ISRAEL

In the past the temptation has been to threaten to launch a military offensive across the Canal if Israel does not promptly withdraw. This type of threat—the threat of deliberate war—is almost certainly counterproductive for the following reasons:

i. Despite Israeli propaganda about how Israel is militarily threatened by Egyptian and Soviet arms, the Israeli government remains convinced that militarily Israel could handle an Egyptian attempt to cross the Canal. The more Egypt talks about renewed formal warfare, the more Israel thinks that that is the problem—and that its military forces can handle it. Further, such talk tends to reinforce the belief of many Israelis that the ultimate Arab objective is to destroy Israel, and to strengthen their tactical conclusion to remain at the Canal, where they can most easily cope with an Egyptian attack.

ii. Some Israelis probably hope for explicit Egyptian threats and military moves that could once again be used to justify an Israeli pre-emptive strike. Israel could effectively use a new war that was blamed on Egypt as superseding Resolution 242 and as demonstrating that it would be absolutely out of the question for Israel to withdraw from the Sinai.

iii. The more that Egypt creates an apparent risk of renewed warfare the more reluctant Israel will be to withdraw, and the less the world will blame Israel for holding its ground. If there appears to be a high risk of open warfare launched by Egypt, it will seem reasonable for Israel to insist that such a war be fought in the vicinity of Suez rather than in the vicinity of Gaza.

The major concern that it is desirable to create in Israel is not over a war deliberately launched by responsible government officials. The concern that Israel ought to feel is rather that over losing an opportunity for real peace and thus condemning itself to a period of indefinite hostility that would erode the democratic and religious principles to which Israel would like to adhere. There is a risk that the attempt to use superior military power to solve the political problems of Jerusalem, the West Bank, and the Sinai will be for Israel what the attempt to use superior military power to solve the political problems of South Vietnam has been for the United States. There is no risk that Palestinian guerrillas will militarily conquer Israel. There is a great risk that the use of military rule to govern by fiat a million people over whom Israel as a Jewish state can make no legitimate claim will gradually sour the confidence of the Israeli people in their own country: They will ask: Are we a Jewish state? Are we a democracy? Do we practice what we preach? One can anticipate that the youth of Israel, like the youth of the United States, will become alienated from their elders. There are major divisions within Israel which could become quite unpleasant if Jewish radicals join Arabs in strikes and demonstrations for freedom, justice, and self-determination. A period of endless hostility without and within, political isolation from most of the countries of the world, criticism like that leveled at South Africa and Rhodesia, diminishing support from Jews in the United States who become increasingly offended by Israeli military rule of people who want to rule themselves, lost self-confidence because Israel does not live up to the principles it professes—a future of that kind is the one that Israelis should worry about if they fail to withdraw from territory that is not theirs.

b. THE SHORT-TERM CONSEQUENCES FOR THE ISRAELI GOVERNMENT

The consequences that government officials most fear are the immediate short-term ones in their own political constituency and among those who give them financial support. A good way to bring pressure on the present Israeli government is to provide opposition leaders and political rivals with the basis for good arguments and criticisms against the present policy. Prime Minister Golda Meir is vulnerable to the charge that she is stubborn, too hostile to compromise, and not sufficiently willing to take risks in the pursuit of a peaceful settlement. The fear that she ought to have is of an increasing political opposition within Israel, which would more and more successfully charge her with being too stubborn: "A good woman for a war, but not for making a peace."

The other consequence that the present leaders of the Israeli government should fear is that of decreasing financial and political support from the Jewish community in the United States. For years Israel has appeared as a tiny, threatened democracy faced with Arab belligerence. A reduced danger of external attack combined with an increased realization that Israel is the one that is unwilling to take steps toward peaceful settlement could well chill the enthusiasm with which some Americans annually contribute to Israel's support. To chill their enthusiasm would certainly require public facts demonstrating the repeated attempts of Egypt to be reasonable (facts so well documented as to be accepted by members of the American Jewish community) and demonstrating the repeated failure of the government of Israel to respond.

2. Strengthening Israeli Hopes of a Real Peace if Israel Does Take the Decisions Proposed

Egypt must have two policies, not one. For the contemplated future actions of Egypt to have any impact on Israel, those actions must be different depending upon what Israel does. If Egypt were to be equally hostile no matter what Israel did, then there would be no point in Israel's trying to do anything to avoid that hostility. Unpleasant consequences that might befall Israel would be seen as the inevitable result of the general situation.

If Israeli citizens and government officials are to be influenced, they must be shown an opportunity for some alternate outcome, a real peace in which they can relax.

In considering what Egypt might do to nurture this confidence that a true peace is within Israel's grasp if only Israel makes the right decisions now, it is necessary to recognize the dual aspect of the problem. The first part of the problem is to figure out what actions would have the most constructive impact on Israel. The second part of the problem is to moderate and present those actions in a manner that takes into account the realities of domestic public opinion in Egypt and elsewhere in the Arab world. The tendency among government officials the world over is to look *only* to domestic opinion, in your case to make statements about Israel that appeal only to Arab opinion.

The consequence within Israel that would have the greatest chance of making withdrawal more likely would be the belief that if, and only if, complete withdrawal took place, Israel would be forgiven, the boycott would end, trade and travel could resume, and a long period of friendly cooperation would be launched. Perhaps not all of this would take place immediately, but before long Israel and Israeli citizens would be freely accepted throughout the Middle East. If every Israeli were convinced of that fact, one could confidently predict that the domestic political pressure upon the Israeli government would be such as to cause it to move toward a peaceful settlement involving complete withdrawal.

It would be politically difficult for an Arab leader suddenly and bluntly to announce that if withdrawal should take place he would pursue a policy of total friendship with Israel. Americans can understand the forces of domestic public opinion. In far less justified circumstances United States leaders thought it politically impossible to establish diplomatic relations and normal trade with China for twenty years after the United States accepted as a fact the existence of the People's Republic. Americans should understand how much more difficult it would be for Egyptian leaders to propose diplomatic relations and normal trade with Israel, which has twice struck Egypt with military force and is currently occupying a large area of Egyptian territory.

Nevertheless, the task of convincing Israeli leaders and Israeli citizens that they now have a chance for a real peace—the kind of peace they want and a peace that would be totally different from what would happen if they refuse to withdraw—is absolutely essential if Egyptian policy is to be successful. The United States cannot be relied upon to impose a settlement on Israel against the weight of Israeli opinion any more than it could impose a settlement upon South Vietnam against the weight of that country's public opinion. To convince Israel that it has a chance for real peace—a chance it had better not miss—will require a carefully worked out strategy based on honest dealing with the public in both Israel and Egypt. Without suddenly upsetting the public, or causing them to doubt the sincerity of the government's statements, Egypt should pursue a policy that will reach and influence Israeli public opinion. In respect to devising such a policy, a few ideas may deserve consideration:

a. DISTINGUISH BETWEEN THE POLICIES OF ISRAELI GOVERNMENT LEADERS AND "THE PEOPLE OF ISRAEL"

If Israel is going to be influenced, more and more Israelis will have to criticize the present policies of their government. Some Israeli citizens and political leaders will have to side with Egypt, favoring what Egypt favors, if the Israeli government is going to be persuaded to do what Egypt wants. Egypt should not insist that all Israeli citizens are bad, or that all Israeli citizens are "enemies." The government of North Vietnam pursues a more effective tactic —it repeatedly indicates that it is fighting Americans only because of the mistaken policies of their leaders. Americans who disagreed with their government's policy were frequently invited to Hanoi and provided with the extra weight and attention accorded those who have talked with the other side.

Speeches critical of Israel should be narrowly focused on specific actions of the Israeli government or perhaps on those of the Prime Minister or the Cabinet. Without losing credibility by exaggerating differences that exist, it would be easy to attack "the Meir policy" of holding on to Arab lands, and this would be better than verbally attacking Israel as a whole. Israeli citizens identify themselves with Israel, and would feel that they personally were being attacked. They are less likely to insist that an attack on Golda Meir is an attack on them.

Individual Israeli citizens, including journalists and public figures, who have been critics of their government's policies should be invited to visit Egypt. Such visits would go far to demonstrate that Egypt is not anti-Jewish, and they would help kindle the hope that all Israelis could expect to live in peace with Egypt once a fair peace had been worked out. Both the political feasibility and the political rewards of such invitations are demonstrated by the invitation extended two years ago by Egypt to the Zionist leader, Nahum Goldmann—even though that visit never took place. A general announcement of a policy change might be made along the following lines:

DRAFT 1
Announcement That Some Israelis Will Be Allowed to Visit Egypt

The government of Egypt today announced that it would receive applications for visas from Israeli citizens who are genuinely interested in promoting peace on a basis of the full implementation of Security Council Resolution 242 of November 22, 1967.

In making the announcement the Minister of Foreign Affairs said:

> We have no quarrel with the Jewish people. We have no quarrel with those Israeli citizens who recognize that if they want to live in peace on Israeli territory, Israel must allow Egyptians to live in peace on Egyptian territory—all of it. We have a serious quarrel with the present Israeli government, which has stubbornly held Egyptian and other Arab lands for more than four years while talking of respect for the rights of others; which subjects a million Arabs to military rule while claiming to be a democracy; and which rejects every peace initiative proposed by us or by the United Nations.

Individual Israeli citizens wishing to apply for a visa to visit Egypt may do so through the Egyptian consulate in Beirut, from which the necessary forms may be obtained. Those applying should be prepared to indicate some disagreement with the policy of the present Israeli government.

Although all Israeli citizens are technically enemy aliens so long as the period of belligerency continues, the government of Egypt will treat any Israeli granted a visa as it would any other foreign visitor and guarantees that he will be as free to come and go as if he were a citizen of a country at peace with Egypt.

Egypt has been effective in maintaining among its citizens a feeling of warmth and friendship for individual United States citizens while severely and openly criticizing policies of the United States government. If all American citizens were barred from Egypt, it would be far more difficult to move United States policy toward that even-handed justice to which Egypt is entitled. It would be equally wise for Egypt to move toward a similar policy regarding Israeli citizens, at least to the extent that individual citizens of Israel who want their government to withdraw its forces from Arab territory can feel that they can look forward to personal friendship and respect, and not to being attacked for policies of which they disapprove.

b. DISTINGUISH BETWEEN PRESENT EGYPTIAN POLICIES AND WHAT WILL HAPPEN ONCE WITHDRAWAL HAS TAKEN PLACE

Just as every government has contingent military plans to be put into effect should war break out, it is appropriate to have contingent peace plans to be put into effect in the event that peace breaks out. One way to give more reality to talk about peace without making "concessions" is to identify things that will be different once withdrawal has taken place and once a fair process for dealing with the Palestinians has been undertaken. Some terms of peace, such as passage of Israeli ships through the Suez Canal, are specified in Resolution 242. Others, though perhaps assumed, are not. It would be useful to go through all current restrictions within Egypt applicable to Israel, Israeli citizens, or Jews and to identify those that ought to be revised or abolished following a peaceful settlement of the major issues of the Arab-Israeli conflict. With careful handling of the domestic public-opinion aspects of the problem, it should be possible to announce changes in restrictions that would take place once Israel withdraws and Resolution 242 is on its way toward full implementation. Perhaps this could be done by announcing that restrictions were being removed immediately for certain Israelis who had already indicated that they were not enemies of Egypt, and by announcing that restrictions would be removed later for all Israeli citizens.

c. MAKE FUTURE POLICIES CREDIBLE BY PROVIDING DETAIL

The task is not simply to provide hopes for Israeli citizens of what *might* happen if Israel withdraws; it is to be so convincing that most Israelis will want to take the risks of withdrawal in order to achieve a peace that looks so probable. One way to do this is to prepare now the actual documents that will govern future policies. Working now on something that you hope will happen later makes it look as though you are taking seriously the possibility that it will happen.

Another way to lend credibility to future contingent plans for peace is to publish now an operational document that will come into effect at a later time, if Israel decides as you would like. One example of this approach would be to have the Egyptian government write to an international airline, authorizing it to work out arrangements for one direct daily round-trip flight between Cairo and Tel Aviv, which could be inaugurated once Israel had withdrawn its forces from the Sinai behind the 1920 international boundary. Such an authorization might be worded along the lines of the following rough draft:

DRAFT 2

Egyptian Authorization of Direct Cairo–Tel Aviv Flights upon Israeli Withdrawal from Sinai

President
Air France
Paris, France
Dear Sir:

Although the future of the Middle East conflict is far from certain, we are hoping that Israeli forces will soon withdraw from all territory occupied in 1967, that other elements of the Security Council Resolution of November 22, 1967, will be fully implemented, and that peace with justice will be established.

We should be ready for peace, just as we are ready for war. Looking forward to that time, I hereby invite Air France to negotiate arrangements with us and with Israel that would permit a daily direct flight each way between Cairo and Tel Aviv. These negotiations could begin immediately, and the flights themselves, so far as we are concerned, could be inaugurated as soon as Israeli armed forces have withdrawn from those portions of Egyptian territory that they occupied in 1967. The air service could be expanded and additional measures of cooperation might be instituted after other elements of the Security Council Resolution are implemented.

In following up this invitation, you should get in touch with Mr. _____ of the Ministry of _____.

Sincerely yours,

_____

(Government of Egypt)

The temptation in drawing up any such letter will be to include all the conditions one could reasonably ask for, such as withdrawal from *all* Arab lands occupied in 1967 and the restoration to the Palestinians of all their rights. For such a letter to be politically effective, however, the condition should be clear, simple, and attainable. Other carrots can be held out for other decisions.

Similar documents could be drawn up dealing with direct telephone and cable communication, financial claims of Jews who had left Egypt, and the phasing out of the boycott. All of such documents might have a built-in terminal date—for example, one year—at which time the effectiveness of the document would expire if withdrawal had not taken place. Operative acts of this kind are far better public relations than speeches and pamphlets devoted to self-praise.

It is difficult during periods of hostility to concentrate on the political weapon of making credible the conditions of peace, but it is important to do so. During World War II the Allies spent a lot of time at Potsdam softening the demand of "unconditional surrender." By defining with some specificity the terms on which the war could end—and by making clear that peace was attractive —the Potsdam Proclamation played a significant role in influencing the Japanese government to opt for peace.[14] Defining peace in terms attractive to Israel can help influence the government of Israel to choose peace instead of a period of protracted hostility.

3. Formulating Proposed Decisions

The formulating of possible decisions the government of Israel might make in order to enjoy the "carrot" of peace rather than the "stick" of protracted hostility is the single most critical aspect of a political campaign. Israel is apparently willing to let the present military occupation continue indefinitely, while it proceeds within Jerusalem, within the West Bank, within Sharm el Sheikh and elsewhere to "change the facts." Egypt is the one that wants decisions to be made. Decisions are more likely to be made if they have been put on the agenda. The decisions Egypt wants made are not likely to be on the agenda unless Egypt formulates them and puts them there. Egypt did advance the proposal that the Suez Canal might be opened as a step toward full implementation of Resolution 242, and that item then became an important one on the international agenda.

In considering the political impact of proposed decisions it is important to recognize two crucial differences between some proposals and others. One is the difference between a general idea and a specific decision. The other is the difference between a specific decision that produces a statement and one that produces tangible results. In the present situation Egypt should try to propose not just ideas, but specific decisions, and not just any specific decisions but ones that, if made, will produce tangible results.

It is the latter kind of specific proposal that I call a "yesable proposition." First, it is sufficiently specific so that it can be answered with the single word *yes*. Second, it is sufficiently palatable so that we might reasonably expect an affirmative answer. And third, it is sufficiently operational so that if an affirmative answer is obtained, we can expect that something we want to have happen will actually happen.

One further important feature of formulating proposed decisions should be borne in mind—that of limiting the time within which an answer is required. Decisions are most likely to be produced if there is not only an item on the agenda but also a limited time within which to act. Ideally, each proposed decision should be seen as a fading opportunity. It is best if the deadline for decision is not one that is arbitrarily asserted (and that can just as easily be extended) but one that is related to outside events such as upcoming elections, the next session of the General Assembly, a relevant season of the year, and so forth. Although a fading opportunity for decision is frequently difficult if not impossible to arrange, an endless opportunity for decision usually produces delay: Those faced with the choice know that they can always decide later and that something better may turn up in the meantime.

Before some particular decisions are discussed, it may be well to weigh the pros and cons of advancing more than one proposal. Undoubtedly, within Israel there is the argument that the policy of holding on to the occupied territory is working. "Egypt," the argument goes, "was reluctant to accept the existence of Israel three years ago. Now Egypt is advancing peace proposals. After perhaps ten more years of occupation Egypt and the other Arab states will become so reasonable that they will make peace with us while letting us keep much of the occupied territory." Those within Egypt who oppose the advancing of any more proposals see doing so as a sign of weakness. And there is no doubt that if Egyptian proposals become increasingly generous as to the terms of a final settlement, Israel will be encouraged to wait for still better terms. But there is no reason for all new proposals to be on the same subject or to constitute a steadily increasing price that Egypt is prepared to pay for withdrawal. Nor need any proposal depart from the substance of the final settlement as provided in Resolution 242.

The best policy for Egypt is to build up political pressure by convincing both Israelis and Americans that the policy of the government of Israel is too intransigent. Such conviction will not be brought about by Israel's having rejected one proposal. The wisest strategy would seem to be to construct a series of specific operational proposals and offer them one after another. If the proposals are fair and reasonable, a series of negative answers by Israel can be expected to produce an accumulating opinion in Israel and in the United States that the present Israeli policy is one of arbitrary stubbornness which merits little support. Each proposal need not be a decision that is increasingly favorable to Israel, but rather one that is fair and sensible—and one that Prime Minister Meir must accept or reject. The proposals may concern different subjects, and may be advanced concurrently. Some may be advanced directly by Egypt. The cumulative effect would be better if some were advanced by third parties, such as the United States or Ambassador Jarring.

Let me now turn to some of the particular decisions that Egypt has been demanding or might ask for.

a. A PROMISE OF TOTAL WITHDRAWAL

Egypt has recognized that it could not expect Israeli withdrawal from occupied territories prior to the working out of other aspects of the comprehensive settlement contemplated in Resolution 242. It has also recognized that although an Israeli promise of total withdrawal is not a fair substitute for withdrawal itself, such a promise would make eventual withdrawal more likely. Egypt has therefore asked Israel for a promise now to withdraw from all of the Sinai, once adequate security arrangements are worked out. Should Egypt continue to press for such a promise? My conclusion is *no*.

First, the more Egypt presses for a promise that Israel withdraw from the Sinai the more Egypt strengthens everyone's impression that if Israel does not promise it does not have to withdraw.

Second, the advantages of such a promise may not be as great as might be supposed. Although the request for a promise is a request for a specific decision, it is not a request for an operational decision. Having made a promise, Israel might find it even easier to stall for time. It could insist that it had promised to withdraw once proper conditions existed—so that no one should press it on that score—and that now the rest of the world would simply have to wait until arrangements were produced that, in Israel's view, guaranteed its security. One could expect that it might be a long time before Israel was satisfied.

Finally, the Israeli Cabinet has decided *not* to make such a promise.[15] Egypt is unlikely in the near future to obtain a flat reversal of that decision, both because governments find it difficult to reverse decisions that they have made and because, from the Israeli point of view, there is much merit in the decision.

From the point of view of Israel the essence of the settlement contemplated in Security Council Resolution 242 of November 22, 1967, is a credit transaction. Israel is being asked to withdraw its force from territories occupied in 1967 and to rely on Arab promises—promises to live in peace with Israel for years to come. In Israeli eyes the Arab credit rating is not very high. Whatever may be the facts of the 1957 understanding about the Gulf of Aqaba and the 1970 understanding about not moving SAM missiles into the Suez Canal Zone during the cease-fire, the widespread impression within Israel is that Egyptian promises must be treated with skepticism. Before Israel is willing to commit itself to withdrawal Israelis would like to see a little more evidence that future promises of Egypt to live in peace with Israel are likely to be kept.

Also, Israel can easily justify not promising to withdraw in the following way: "So long as there is a risk of war, let it be at Suez rather than Gaza. And even if we are to withdraw completely (about which there is a great difference of opinion), our chance of getting good security arrangements within the Sinai will be better if we use total withdrawal in bargaining for security arrangements than if we first commit ourselves to total withdrawal."

In going forward on other matters Egypt can avoid accepting the Israeli position that it will *not* withdraw from occupied territories by making a statement along the following lines:

DRAFT 3

Egyptian Statement on Total Withdrawal

We believed that a promise of complete withdrawal would have been helpful by resolving the debate over whether Resolution 242 means withdrawal from "all territories occupied in 1967" as we contend or whether it means withdrawal from "some territories occupied in 1967" as others have suggested. An Israeli promise of complete withdrawal, like a debtor's promise to pay his debts, is by no means essential. What is important is performance. It is clear that before actual implementation of Resolution 242 can take place arrangements will have to be worked out to guarantee our security and Israel's security across the Sinai boundary. Work should proceed promptly on the actual drafting of such security arrangements so that the Meir government will have no excuse for failing to withdraw as provided for by the Security Council. If eventually we are unable to agree upon whether the Security Council resolution calls for total withdrawal or not, the Security Council itself will have to decide.

It seems unwise to continue to press Israel for a promise of total withdrawal. Israel should now be asked to make some other decisions.

b. THE SUEZ CANAL PROPOSAL

The Egyptian proposal for partial withdrawal from the Sinai and for opening the Suez Canal as an interim step toward full implementation of Resolution 242 was an astute political initiative. The proposal put the subject on the agenda, and it demonstrated Egypt's interest in moving toward a peaceful settlement. It was not, however, a specific proposal to which the word *yes* would have been an adequate answer; certainly an affirmative answer would not have produced operational results. The proposal was more in the form of an idea: How about opening the Canal pursuant to an interim agreement along the following lines? Discussion during the ensuing months has demonstrated that Israel can move slowly and make countersuggestions without incurring as much political cost as Egypt would like.

It is in Egypt's interest that the Canal be opened and that Israeli ships be allowed to go through it, so that Egypt can demonstrate to Israeli and world public opinion that it is serious about making peace with Israel provided that its territory is returned. Full performance by Egypt of its promises pursuant to an interim agreement will help re-establish Egypt's credit rating. Paying some "cash in advance" and fully performing on some modest promises will help convince Israelis that Arab promises of full peace in exchange for full withdrawal are sincere and can be relied upon.

Under these circumstances it is unwise to insist upon an Israeli promise of eventual total withdrawal as a condition to agreeing upon opening the Canal in exchange for partial withdrawal. The only necessity is that Egypt not abandon or weaken its position that the Security Council resolution should be fully implemented and that that resolution requires total withdrawal, at least in so far as the Sinai is concerned.

To maximize the chance of Israel's accepting the Egyptian suggestion of an interim agreement on the Canal it is necessary to maximize the political cost to Israel of not accepting. This is best done by converting the suggestion into a specific, operational, "yesable proposition" put to Israel by a third party with maximum legitimacy and maximum international support.

One of the ways to convert the idea into an operational proposal would be to write a letter to the United States, containing the operational language necessary to govern the opening of the Canal and the limitations that Egypt would be willing to assume with respect to the portion of the Sinai from which Israel had withdrawn. Here is an illustrative draft of such a letter:

DRAFT 4
Egyptian Letter on Partial Withdrawal and the Suez Canal

The Honorable William P. Rogers
Secretary of State
Washington, D.C.
Dear Mr. Secretary:

For some months you have been exploring the possibility of promoting an interim agreement under which Israeli forces would engage in a stage of withdrawal and the Suez Canal might be reopened. You know our deep-seated fears that such an interim agreement would tend to become permanent, and that once the Canal was reopened the world would be even more tolerant of Israel's continued occupation of our territory. You know our view that it is the military equipment provided Israel by the United States which permits Israel to continue to occupy our territory. Nevertheless, to demonstrate the sincerity of our desire for a peaceful settlement, and to give you the kind of assurances you may need in order to justify your withholding further arms from Israel, we are sending you this letter.

If within the next ninety days all members of the Israeli armed forces in the Sinai are withdrawn east of a north-south line that is no less than fifty kilometers from the closest point of the Suez Canal, then the government of Egypt assures you and authorizes you to assure the government of Israel:

1. That less than one thousand military personnel of Egypt or of any other friendly state will be deployed in the Sinai east of the Suez Canal in the area from which Israeli armed forces have been withdrawn

2. That upon the opening of the Suez Canal ships carrying Israeli cargo and ships flying the Israeli flag will be allowed to pass through the Canal on a nondiscriminatory basis

3. That Egypt will observe a cease-fire for a period of no less than one year from the date of this letter

4. That Egypt will designate a liaison officer to meet with one designated by Israel for the purpose of working out arrangements to avoid conflict or misunderstanding along the temporary line between the two forces

We make these assurances to permit a period of peace and cooperation, during which arrangements may be worked out covering other aspects of Security Council Resolution 242 and permitting the full implementation of that resolution. Although we do not now insist that Israel commit itself fully to withdraw from every inch of our territory occupied in 1967, that is our interpretation of Security Council Resolution 242, and it is our position that such withdrawal must take place.

It is contemplated that the interim arrangement governed by these assurances shall be superseded by agreements to be negotiated within the next few months and certainly within one year. If not previously superseded, the assurances shall terminate one year from the date of this letter.

Sincerely yours,

_____

(Government of Egypt)

Such a letter would first confront the United States government with an operational decision—whether it should endorse the letter

—and, if that was affirmative, would then confront the Israeli government with such a decision.

With respect to the Suez Canal proposal it would be desirable to stir up greater awareness in Western Europe of the high price it is paying for leaving the Canal shut. Western Europe alone is probably paying in excess of one million dollars per day for each day that the Canal remains closed. Those countries signatory to the Convention of Constantinople of 1888 have a legal right to go through the Canal. A continuing dispute between Egypt and Israel does not justify closing the Canal and imposing additional costs on Europe. Egypt has a legal argument for closing the Canal to shipping that threatens the security of Egypt[16] (and has accepted the jurisdiction of the International Court of Justice to review that argument),[17] but Israel has no legal basis for interfering with European traffic through the Canal in order to gain advantages for itself.

On July 11, 1971, Foreign Minister Abba Eban was quoted as saying that Israel was prepared to accept an arrangement with respect to the Canal ". . . on condition it was based on a reasonable balance of advantages and not on the principle that the only beneficiary of such an agreement should be Egypt." If possible, the European Common Market or some other spokesman for the consumers of Europe should vigorously and loudly represent their interests. Israel would seem to have no legal or moral right to continue to block the Canal, to the great cost of consumers in Europe and elsewhere, in order to exact "advantages" for itself. This should be made apparent.

c. "DIRECT" FACE-TO-FACE DISCUSSIONS

At some point the issue of face-to-face discussions involving both Arab and Israeli representatives is going to become prominent. If political pressure builds up against Israel, Israel will stress the line: "How can we believe that the Arabs are willing to live in peace with us if they won't even talk with us?" That is an effective political argument that undercuts much of what Egypt has accomplished by its political offensive. It is likely to be effective in the future. Some third parties may themselves call for face-to-face talks.

There are three ways in which Egypt can deal with this issue. First, it can wait until the question is pressed and then refuse to engage in any discussions involving face-to-face meetings with Israeli representatives. Such refusal would be unwise, for several reasons:

- There is no sound principle in support of avoiding face-to-face discussions.
- Egyptian representatives now participate regularly in Security Council and General Assembly meetings that include Israeli representatives.
- In accepting the Rogers initiative in July 1970, Egypt agreed to meetings involving face-to-face discussions with Israeli representatives if Jarring should so recommend.
- To refuse a direct request for such meetings would reduce political pressure on Israel.

The second way in which Egypt can deal with the issue of face-to-face discussions is to wait until the issue is pressed and then agree. This is better than refusing, but is not a very attractive possibility. It is likely to look, both to Israeli and to Arab public opinion, as though Egypt is backing down.

The third and, in my judgment, by far the best way to deal with the issue is to take the offensive. Egypt should distinguish between private, two-party, "direct negotiations" to which Egypt has always been and remains opposed, and meetings at the United Nations, with third parties present, for the purpose of implementing Resolution 242. By taking the lead, Egypt can clarify its past policy and define the kind of meeting to which it does not object.[18]

The reason for moving forward on this issue at this time is not the expectation that discussions involving face-to-face meetings are suddenly going to produce a change in Israel's position. Quite the contrary. The request for such meetings would be directed at weakening Israel's argument that progress will take place once it meets face-to-face to explain its views to Arab spokesmen. Such meetings will also provide Arab representatives a forum for advancing specific suggestions that will either lead to action or demonstrate the "stubbornness" of Prime Minister Meir's policy.

It is Egypt that wants action and it is Egypt that is going to have to produce the initiatives that will increase the cost to Israel of saying no. In proposing face-to-face discussions Egypt should propose a specific topic, such as security arrangements for the Sinai. The following draft illustrates that possibility.

DRAFT 5
Egyptian Letter to the Secretary-General on Face-to-Face Talks

Mr. _____ _____
Secretary-General of the United Nations
New York, New York 10017
Dear Mr. Secretary-General:

As you fully appreciate, it has taken far too long to implement Security Council Resolution 242 of November 22, 1967. Neither Israel's refusal to commit itself to the full implementation of that resolution nor the fact that the United States has been exploring the possibility of an interim arrangement with respect to the Suez Canal justifies reduced efforts by the United Nations. Quite the contrary. The less responsibility Israel is willing to undertake toward implementing the resolution, the more responsibility others must undertake. The United Nations, and in particular your Special Representative, Ambassador Jarring, should move forthwith to prepare those documents necessary to implement Resolution 242.

Requiring urgent attention are the security arrangements to govern the region of the Sinai boundary between Israel and Egypt following the withdrawal of Israeli forces. We hereby request that you or Ambassador Jarring prepare, in consultation with the parties, operational documents, in the form of a Security Council resolution, and draft agreements between Egypt and Israel, and among the guaranteeing powers, to provide both Israel and Egypt with reasonable assurance that the other will not launch hostile military action during or following the withdrawal of Israeli forces from the Sinai. We believe that the documents should be in such form that should Israel be unwilling to withdraw its forces despite the assurance of reasonable security arrangements, the Security Council could then on its own authority put the measures into effect and require the withdrawal.

In their acceptances of Secretary Rogers' initiative of June 19, 1970, both Israel and Egypt committed themselves to designating representatives to discussions to be held under Ambassador Jarring's auspices according to such procedure and at such places and times as he might recommend, taking into account as appropriate each side's preference as to method of procedure and the previous experience between the parties.

As you know, Egypt has long been convinced that the estab- lishment of peace and justice in the Middle East is a task that requires both respect for the standards of international law and the active participation of representatives of the international community to assure such respect and to assure full justice for the Palestinian people. Our territory has been taken by force and is now being held by force despite the unanimous action of the Security Council "Emphasizing the inadmissibility of the acquisi- tion of territory by war" and affirming "that the fulfillment of Charter principles requires . . . Withdrawal of Israeli armed forces from territories occupied in the recent [1967] conflict."

One does not go into a closet with an armed thief to negotiate about the return of stolen property. Under these circumstances we have been and remain opposed to so-called direct negotiations that consist of private two-party talks, without international stand- ards and without international participation to see that those standards are respected.

We have regularly met with Israeli representatives in the Security Council and in the General Assembly. We do not object in principle to Israeli participation in meetings with our representatives. Despite Israeli charges to the contrary, we have not been and are not now unwilling to meet face to face with Israeli representatives at the United Nations for the purpose of implementing the Security Council resolution with the participation of your representative or other appropriate international representatives.

To move forward as rapidly as possible, and to put to rest the Israeli suggestion that if only we would listen to them, all our problems would be solved, we request that Ambassador Jarring immediately convene discussions at the United Nations for the purpose of drafting actual texts of security arrangements to govern the period during and after Israeli withdrawal from the Sinai, and that some of the sessions devoted to this work include, along with Ambassador Jarring, representatives of both Egypt and Israel.

We urge you to request Ambassador Jarring to proceed with the drafting of security arrangements whether or not Israel accepts an invitation to participate. We are as skeptical of Israeli intentions as they purport to be of ours. The people of Israel have legitimate interests that deserve consideration. That does not mean, however, that the present Israeli cabinet should be allowed to exercise a veto over the Security Council resolution or over all efforts to implement it.

We look forward to hearing from you or from Ambassador Jarring in the immediate future.

Sincerely yours,

_____

(Government of Egypt)

d. SECURITY ARRANGEMENTS IN THE SINAI

Whatever is done now about face-to-face talks, something should be done to press forward in producing a clear plan for dealing with the security problem—for assuring Israel and Egypt of the unlikelihood of military attack by the other. Israel has a strong case for postponing any withdrawal until demilitarized zones or other means of assuring territorial inviolability have been worked out. Since Egypt has accepted the principle of demilitarized zones in accepting Resolution 242, Egypt can hardly expect Israel to withdraw before some kind of demilitarized or security zone has been put down on paper and offered to it.

Through the Jarring talks the parties could agree to establish a working subcommittee and agree on instructions to it, spelling out the principles that should guide its task. Below is a draft illustrating this approach.

DRAFT 6
Memorandum of Agreement:
Working Subcommittee of the Jarring
Talks on Security

1. A subcommittee of the Jarring discussions shall be established immediately to prepare nonbinding drafts of operational documents for security arrangements in the Sinai area. The subcommittee shall be composed of a chairman designated by Ambassador Jarring, and two to three members each designated by the governments of Israel and Egypt.

2. The subcommittee shall submit for consideration within ninety days the following operational draft documents consistent with the guidelines and principles enumerated below:

—An agreement between Israel and Egypt on security measures
—A Security Council resolution
—Any other agreement, undertaking, resolution, or document

related to guarantees and security in the Sinai or mutual
security between Israel and Egypt which the subcommittee
believes desirable

The subcommittee may submit alternative or variant drafts consistent with the enumerated principles if it deems this appropriate
or is unable to submit drafts reflecting a consensus.

3. Members of the subcommittee shall meet with the chairman
and, as the work progresses, in informal sessions with other
members of the subcommittee as the chairman deems most useful
for completing the work.

4. Operational drafts prepared by the subcommittee shall be
sufficient to govern all arrangements—including level, status, and
limitation on military forces and other personnel—necessary to
ensure local security within the Sinai and a high degree of mutual
security in the Sinai area and along the boundaries between
Israel and Egypt both during and after withdrawal of Israeli forces
in accordance with Resolution 242.

In particular, drafts shall govern:
—Security arrangements during withdrawal of Israeli forces
—Establishment, operation, maintenance, and termination of
    security zones
—Rules applicable within security zones
—Arrangements for causing compliance and for dealing with
    noncompliance with such rules
—Procedures for settling disputes
—Procedures for revising arrangements should that later prove
    advisable

5. Principles: Drafts prepared by the subcommittee shall be
consistent with the following principles:

a. The withdrawal of Israeli forces as provided in Security
Council Resolution 242 shall take place in stages.

b. The fact that some Israeli forces shall be withdrawn more quickly than others shall not delay establishment of security zones in areas where, during a transitional period, some Israeli forces remain.

c. In any security zone where Israeli personnel are present during a transitional period there shall be present military control units of both parties under specified conditions and limitations.

d. There shall be present in security zones international control units that are to be authorized by the Security Council and that are to include personnel of third states.

e. International control personnel shall be given authority to deal with problems that may arise and to make recommendations with which local personnel of both parties shall comply unless and until they later receive contrary orders from their own government at a high level.

f. There shall be provisions limiting and governing the taking of self-help action by either government.

e. THE GULF OF AQABA

Although the willingness of Egypt to assure freedom of navigation for Israeli shipping in the Gulf of Aqaba, like the willingness of Israel to withdraw from Sharm el Sheikh, depends upon progress on a number of other questions, the substance of an agreement about Aqaba and the Strait of Tiran can be worked out quite independently. It is to the interest of Egypt to remove all dispute about freedom of passage through the Strait of Tiran and the Gulf of Aqaba. The clearer Israel's rights to use the waterway are the easier it will be to assure that those rights will be respected and the less reason Israel will have for staying at Sharm el Sheikh.

One might think that since passage through the Gulf is more important for Israel than for Egypt this question should be left for Israel to press. Quite the contrary. There is really no dispute about the goal of a peaceful settlement so far as the Gulf of Aqaba is concerned. Israeli ships and shipping should have all reasonable rights of access. Aqaba is therefore a subject on which Egypt can go forward without fear of prejudicing the final outcome. In preparing drafts concerning Aqaba Egypt can demonstrate its peaceful intentions and its reasonableness without having to go beyond Resolution 242. Egypt can dangle the carrots of peace in front of the Israeli public, it can make those carrots seem credible and attractive, without having to make any concessions—without having to concede more carrots than were already provided for in Resolution 242.

Egypt should probably work out for its private use alternative drafts of the substantive and procedural rules it might like to see in effect governing the Gulf of Aqaba and the Strait of Tiran. It might well be better not to table such drafts at the outset, but rather to get a procedure started by means of which such drafts might be considered and revised. One way would be to write a letter to the Secretary-General's Special Representative along the following lines:

DRAFT 7
Egyptian Letter Suggesting a Subcommittee Work on the Gulf of Aqaba

His Excellency, Dr. Gunnar Jarring
Special Representative of the Secretary-General
United Nations
New York, New York
Dear Mr. Ambassador:

As you know, we believe that work toward implementing the Security Council resolution of November 1967 should proceed concurrently on a number of different issues if all the arrangements that must be worked out are going to be resolved within the foreseeable future. One issue on which work could now proceed is the question of access to and transit through and over the Strait of Tiran and the Gulf of Aqaba.

Security Council Resolution 242 affirms the necessity for guaranteeing freedom of navigation through international waterways in the area. Such guarantees involve three elements:

First, establishment of the substantive rules. Although there appears to be no major dispute as to the rules that should be established for the Strait of Tiran and the Gulf of Aqaba, there may well be problems in dealing with such questions as the rights of merchant ships and warships of nonlittoral states, the rights of aircraft in regard to flight over the Gulf, and the precise meaning of "innocent passage."

The second element is to establish procedures for dealing with questions that may come up in the future, arising either from a dispute over questions of law or fact or from a suggestion to revise a rule in the light of experience.

The third element is to establish arrangements that will give the four littoral states and others reasonable assurance that the rules will be respected. We believe that this third element, which involves such questions as those of the military forces at Sharm el Sheikh, should be easier to resolve once substantive and procedural rules governing the Gulf of Aqaba and the Strait of Tiran have been agreed upon.

We hereby suggest that you establish a subcommittee or working party to undertake the work of drafting appropriate documents to govern the Gulf of Aqaba and the Strait of Tiran. We are designating Mr. _____ to work as our representative on this problem with you or with someone designated by you. We are fully aware that not only Israel and Egypt but also Jordan and Saudi Arabia have sovereign interests in the Gulf of Aqaba. The willingness of any state to conclude a binding agreement with respect to the Gulf will undoubtedly depend upon steps that have been or are being taken with respect to other issues in the Middle

East, but there is no reason why the preparatory work of drafting and perhaps initialing the necessary documents governing the Gulf cannot begin immediately.

Sincerely yours,

_____

(Government of Egypt)

f. HELPING PALESTINIANS PARTICIPATE

The legitimate grievances of Palestinians, both as refugees and as a people currently without a political home, constitute a serious problem for the Egyptian government.

Egypt is committed to securing full justice for the Palestinians. The Palestinians have defined for themselves "full justice" in terms of a goal that is wholly unrealistic: Their goal is to abolish the concept of a Jewish homeland and to replace Israel with a democratic state of Palestine in which Christians, Moslems, and Jews would live happily ever after. The Palestinians have also proposed a means for attaining this goal that is equally unrealistic: military action.

Since there is no possibility of the Palestinians achieving in the foreseeable future what they presently consider to be complete victory, the future necessarily involves either compromise or years of frustration—and perhaps both.

Egypt, as the generally acknowledged leader in the Arab world, is currently seen as a major champion of the Palestinian cause. In the absence of unified and effective Palestinian leadership, Egypt is likely to be held responsible for the fate of the Palestinians. It will be politically costly if not politically impossible for Egypt to be the one that accepts a compromise for the Palestinians that falls far short of what they see as their legitimate goal. Far easier for Egypt is to allow the present unhappy situation of the Palestinians to continue, and to accept some responsibility for their continuing frustration. And yet to have the problem continue in its present form is harsh on the Palestinians and makes it difficult to deal effectively with other aspects of the Arab-Israeli conflict.

The Palestinians cannot continue to insist that they have the right to determine their own future, refuse to participate in discussions about that future, and then hold Egypt responsible for what happens. The solution to the Palestinian problem from the point of view of Egypt lies in helping Palestinians accept responsibility for participating in decisions about their own future.

Today there are some Palestinians in Gaza, in Jerusalem, and on the West Bank who would be interested in talking with Israelis and others in order to develop some realistic possibilities. One consideration that deters them is the risk that they will be regarded by Cairo and by other Arab leaders as traitors to the Arab cause. Since it is to the interest of Cairo as well as of the Palestinians that Palestinians do talk with Israelis, Cairo should do what it can to make such discussions more likely.

Most helpful, of course, would be to make clear that Egypt itself is not opposed to all discussions but only to private, two-party talks without guidelines and without international participation. Beyond that, speeches and statements from Cairo could indicate support for those Palestinians willing to wage their own peace offensive. For example, Palestinians on the West Bank could be encouraged to meet with Israeli citizens who have sympathy with the Palestinian problem and could be supported in efforts to draft proposals for Jerusalem or for Gaza or for the West Bank. By one means or another Egypt should make clear that any Palestinian who is willing to deal realistically with Israel and with the future of the Palestinians will not be criticized by Cairo for doing so.

g. USING THE SECURITY COUNCIL

Although Egypt may not have the capability of launching a successful military offensive against Israel, it has strong political support in those institutions that can gradually increase the political—and economic—cost to Israel of pursuing a policy of protracted stubbornness. Simple condemnation in the Security Council will not do much, but the Security Council can do better than that. In all probability the Security Council will again be actively involved in the conflict. Egypt should now set to work thinking about and actually drafting the text of resolutions that the Security Council might adopt. To stimulate your thinking here are ten short drafts, some of which are alternatives to each other, illustrating the kind of action that Egypt might want the Security Council to take. In each case the draft embodies only the operational paragraph or paragraphs of a longer resolution, it being easy to imagine the thrust of the recital clauses.

DRAFT 8
Security Council Resolution Requesting Secretary-General to Prepare Drafts

Requests the Secretary-General, in order to stimulate progress in the discussions taking place through his Special Representative, to prepare alternative drafts of operational documents designed to implement fully Resolution 242.

DRAFT 9
Security Council Resolution Requesting Special Representative to Prepare Drafts

Requests the Secretary-General to have his Special Representative prepare, in consultation with the parties and with members of the Security Council, specific operational proposals, including treaties, agreements, and resolutions, which he would recommend in order fully to implement Security Council Resolution 242, and *Requests* the Special Representative to report such proposals, individually or collectively as appropriate, to the parties and to the Secretary-General.

DRAFT 10

Security Council Resolution Urging
Establishment of Subcommittees

Urges the Special Representative to establish a number of subcommittees of the discussions under his auspices and to ask each
subcommittee to prepare operational recommendations on particular issues involved in implementing Resolution 242, namely:

    (a) Nature and location of security zones and control forces

    (b) Mechanisms for repatriation of refugees

    (c) Form of guarantees of passage through international
        waterways

    (d) Jerusalem, and

Urges the Special Representative to appoint a chairman of each
subcommittee and to request that the parties designate three
representatives each to each subcommittee.

DRAFT 11

Security Council Resolution Requesting Secretary-
General to Study and Report on Alternative
Forms of Guarantees

Requests the Secretary-General, in consultation with his Special
Representative and with the permanent members of the Security
Council, to study alternative forms of guarantees that might be
provided by action of the Security Council and its permanent
members in order to ensure the durability of a Middle East peace
settlement implementing Resolution 242 and the security of all
states in the area, to explore alternative plans for the presence of
foreign, United Nations, or mixed forces in the area as an element

of such guarantees, and to report to the Security Council on the feasibility of such plans.

DRAFT 12

Security Council Resolution Requesting Withdrawal Plans Within Sixty Days

Requests the Secretary-General and his Special Representative, after consultation with the parties and the permanent members of the Security Council, to report within sixty days on:

a. Feasibility of and specific plans for immediate withdrawal of Israeli forces from occupied territories in the Sinai to the lines of June 4, 1967, with such minor rectifications as may be desirable for mutual security

b. Concrete proposals for security arrangements and for guarantees in the Sinai area and along the Sinai border between Egypt and Israel involving international, major power, or mixed forces

c. Detailed plans for accomplishing the withdrawal and at the same time for implementing the security arrangements

d. Detailed plans for opening the Suez Canal and guaranteeing the right of passage through the Canal and Strait of Tiran to ships of all nations, including Israel

e. Proposed documents embodying formal recognition by Egypt and by Israel of the boundary between them

f. Proposed procedures for immediate, direct face-to-face discussions among all the parties to resolve promptly all other issues involved in fully implementing Resolution 242

Provided that upon the Secretary-General's report the Council shall consider whether implementation of this portion of Resolution 242 could take place immediately or should await de-

velopment of similar plans for implementing the balance of the
resolution.

DRAFT 13
Security Council Resolution on
Consulting with Palestinians

Requests the Secretary-General to establish an *ad hoc* committee
of three to consult with Palestinians of all views and to develop
(1) proposals for Palestinian participation in international consideration of questions concerning them and (2) proposals for
peaceful steps toward realization of their inalienable rights.

DRAFT 14
Security Council Resolution on
Return of West Bank Refugees

Requests the government of Israel to increase the rate at which
persons who resided in the West Bank before June 1967 shall be
permitted to return to their homes so that no less than two hundred
per week and no more than one thousand per week shall be
allowed to do so, and
Calls upon the United Nations Relief and Works Agency to
facilitate this process.

DRAFT 15
Security Council Resolution on Return of
Ten Thousand Refugees to Israel

Calls upon Israel to begin at once accepting and processing
applications from Arabs who prior to May 14, 1948, resided in
territory that is within the June 4, 1967, boundaries of Israel and

to readmit for permanent residence within the next twelve months
no less than ten thousand persons who fit that category, *provided that* such persons may be required to affirm that they accept
Israeli citizenship and commit themselves to live peacefully within
Israel, reserving their right to seek changes in the Israeli government only through peaceful political processes, and
Calls upon Israel to cooperate with the United Nations Relief and
Works Agency in compiling statistics on those making such
applications, and on those accepted, rejected, and deferred.

DRAFT 16

Security Council Resolution on Israeli Construction in Occupied Territory

Calls upon the government of Israel to refrain at once from beginning any new construction of Jewish residences in occupied
territories.
Declares that all residential and other construction undertaken
by Israel after June 5, 1967, in East Jerusalem or elsewhere in
Arab territory under Israeli military occupation shall be available
for the rehousing of Palestinian refugees, that the construction by
Israel of housing or other buildings on territory occupied in 1967
in no way confers any legal or equitable rights to the continued
Jewish use of such buildings or land, but that the value of such
buildings shall be taken into account in agreements on
compensation.

There has been increasing recognition of the problem of Israel's
extracting petroleum from the Sinai while holding the territory
under military occupation. Egypt might want to consider raising
this issue at the Security Council and seeking a resolution concerning it. The following are a few ideas:

DRAFT 17
Security Council Resolution on Extracting
Petroleum from the Sinai

Finds that the extraction of petroleum from the Sinai by Israel is a seizure of capital property contrary to the international law of military occupation.

Orders the government of Israel to cease immediately the extraction of petroleum or other minerals from any territory subject to its military occupation as a result of the conflict of June 1967.

Determines that Egypt is entitled to financial compensation for all petroleum heretofore or hereafter extracted from the Sinai by or with the authorization of the government of Israel.

Warns Israel that should it continue to extract petroleum in defiance of the Security Council's decision, the Council will consider authorizing any member of the United Nations to destroy the petroleum extraction facilities located by Israel in the Sinai.

This long letter covers much ground. I hope it convinces you that Egypt has a great many more choices than the simple one of doing nothing or going to war. Either of those alternatives is likely to lead to disaster. The drafts and ideas suggested hold no promise of quick success, nor are they by any means the best that could be produced, but the approach at least holds more promise than does that of doing nothing or going to war.

With the thought that this letter contains ideas of possible interest to a wider audience, I am planning to publish it (with your name omitted) together with comparable letters that I have written to others involved in the Middle East problem. Needless to say, there is no implication that you or anyone else agrees with anything that I have written.

I am also sending you, under separate cover, copies of the letters I have written to others. I recognize that it is most unusual for anyone to look at a conflict first from one point of view and then from another, offering suggestions to each party as to how best to pursue its interests. There is a terrible pressure on one to "take sides." Participants find it hard to believe that they might be better served by one who does not take sides. But neither side will pursue peaceful means unless it can see them as a way of advancing its own interests. Each is benefited if the other can be persuaded to take an enlightened view of its self-interest.

If you have any reactions, criticisms, or comments I would obviously welcome them.

With warm personal regards,

ROGER FISHER

3.
Letter to an Israeli

August 17, 1971

Dear ———— [an official of the government of Israel],

Some time back you suggested I write you a letter pulling together conclusions that I thought applicable to Israel and its role in the Arab-Israeli conflict. Our more recent discussions convinced me that I should try my hand at such a letter, even though you may think it too long.

Ends and Means

The most important question to answer is what questions are important. Those of you with responsibility for what happens have only a limited amount of time and energy. One can, with profit, criticize the past conduct of Arab leaders, United States officials, the Soviet Union, Ambassador Jarring, or the Security Council. We should learn from our past mistakes. But in allocating intellectual resources I am convinced that within the Israeli government, as within other governments, a greater portion should now be devoted to the questions, Where do we go next? and How do we propose to get there from here?

As seen from the outside, Israel's present policy is easily explicable and easily justified. Four elements stand out.

1. Retain the occupied territories so long as there is a risk of war with the Arab states. If there is going to be military action let it take place on Arab land far from Jerusalem and Tel Aviv.

2. Preserve issues that might be useful in eventual bargaining with the Arabs. Whatever amount of the Arab territory is to be returned, Israel should make no promise to withdraw except· in exchange for real concessions from the Arabs. In the same way, Israel should neither compensate some refugees nor allow others to return to Israel except in exchange for Arab concessions negotiated in advance.

3. Don't rush into a settlement. The passage of time will change the facts. New apartments around Jerusalem, hotels in Sharm el Sheikh, oil developments in the Sinai, and new kibbutzim on the Golan Heights will all operate to strengthen Israel's hand in such bargaining as may eventually take place. The longer the occupation continues, the happier the Arabs will be to get any territory back.

4. Recognize and make clear the Soviet threat. The Soviet presence in the Mediterranean is real and probably permanent. Both Israeli and American public opinion will more easily support a government that is standing up to the Soviet Goliath than one seen as needing military power to face only the Arabs.

This policy has a further advantage in that it does not force a division within the Israeli government. Although there are quite diverse views within the government, most can support a government that makes no concessions to the Arabs or to anybody else.

Although easily justified and explained as a response to the actions of others, Israel's present course is less easily defended as the best way of getting to where Israel would like to be some years hence. In the short term—as always—attention must be given to military security. But to devote exclusive attention to the short term and to military security is likely to leave Israel with no long-term answer—and no real security.

Today, I believe, Israel is in danger of becoming a country without a dream—without a goal toward which it is striving. Israel sees itself as a democratic Jewish state that wants to live in peace with its Arab neighbors. But on close inspection, the goal becomes fuzzy. The basic, uncomfortable fact is that Israel cannot keep the occupied territories, recognize that their Arab inhabitants have full democratic rights, and at the same time remain a Jewish state.

Israel can justify its holding of the occupied territories for the time being for reasons of military security and for purposes of future bargaining, but does Israel want to keep the territory permanently? Or does Israel want to return the occupied territory? What is the long-term goal for a democratic Jewish state with a million Arabs under military rule without democratic rights? Some Israelis would like to incorporate all the occupied territories as part of Israel. Some would favor giving full citizenship rights to all the Arabs. Others would like to see them leave, and might be willing to hasten that process. Some would like a small Israel that is more purely Jewish. Some favor a larger Israel that is less Jewish or less democratic or less respectful of the interests of Arabs. But Israel cannot have the maximum of all three elements involved here: territory, democracy, and retention of its Jewish character.

Faced with this dilemma the Israeli government has taken the easy way out: Avoid clarifying the goal, and just handle the problems day by day. There is a tendency to justify each day's decisions not as reasonable steps toward a desirable future but rather as pragmatic responses to the misdeeds of others. This is a dangerous course. Pragmatism is a necessary but not a sufficient ingredient for the policy of any state. Israel needs its idealism. To keep the support and enthusiasm of its people it needs to be seen as pursuing laudable goals by legitimate means. And in the long term, the only way to be seen to be doing that is to do it.

The military occupation of Arab territory runs the risk of being for Israel what Vietnam has been for the United States. There are, of course, drastic differences. Vietnam is used not to prove the point, but to illustrate the character and quality of risks that Israel may be running to the extent that it relies on military force to deal with what is essentially a political problem, and to the extent that it measures the legitimacy of that force by its own perception of the illegitimacy of the force used against it.

The most probable danger for Israel is not a military defeat by an organized army. A more likely danger is that increasingly the Israeli people and Jews throughout the world will lose confidence in the rightness of Israel's cause. Questions concerning the long-term objectives of Israel can be expected to become more apparent. As military occupation drags on, doubts will be raised about both its ends and its means. Palestinian claims that Arabs as well as Jews have a right to self-determination can be expected to find increasing support among Israeli intellectuals. Israeli military forces reported that between July 1 and August 10, 1971, they had killed twenty-five Arab guerrillas in Gaza. Israel could not hope to solve the Palestinian problem by killing every misguided Arab any more than the United States could hope to solve the Vietcong problem by killing every misguided Vietnamese. If the Israeli military should follow the American precedent of reporting a body count—and of considering a dead guerrilla as a measure of success rather than a measure of failure—perhaps they should expect results not unlike those we found in Vietnam: increasing opposition among our adversaries and increasing doubts among our people and our friends.

One of the first warning signs of what Vietnam was doing to the United States was the unwillingness of some young men to serve in the Army. In August 1971 the following item appeared in the *New York Times:*

4 Israelis Won't Serve;
Term Army 'Occupying'
TEL AVIV, Aug. 3 (AP)—Three Israeli men and a woman said today they had sent their draft notices back to Defense Minister Moshe Dayan with a letter saying they were not ready to "serve in an occupying army."

A Defense Ministry spokesman said the letter had not yet reached the ministry but declined to comment on possible consequences of the move. It is rare for a political motive to be cited in Israel as grounds for seeking to avoid military service.

The letter said in part, "We were not born free in order to become oppressors and oppression is not a good reason to die."

Another similarity between United States policy toward Vietnam and Israeli policy toward the Arabs lies in the approach toward "negotiations." In my view the negotiations over Vietnam in Paris have been in large part a charade, put on for the benefit of spectators and public opinion. The United States government essentially believed that its adversaries were "not ready for serious negotiations" and that more time would have to pass before they were. Speeches were made and positions taken in Paris not with the expectation of reaching an agreement but rather with the aim of demonstrating to third states and to public opinion at home that we had tried. This process further undercut public confidence in the credibility of the government and in its genuine desire for a peaceful settlement. The fact that our Vietnamese adversaries may have been equally cynical did not offset the damage.

Israel's approach toward the Jarring talks is comparable. Israel believes that its adversaries are "not ready for serious negotiations." Positions are taken in the Jarring talks with little or no expectation of reaching an agreement. Such negotiations may be expected to undercut confidence in the Israeli government and in its genuine desire for a peaceful settlement. The fact that Arab governments are equally skeptical of accomplishing anything through negotiations may not offset the damage.

This is not a prediction of what is necessarily going to happen, or even of what is most probable. Rather, it is the identification of a plausible risk that the Israeli government should take into account. The risk may be both more likely than that of a major war launched by the Arab states and—should it materialize—more damaging to Israel. The risk may become greater with the passage of time.

Many Israelis have concluded that "time is on Israel's side." They point out that with the passage of time the Arab position is prejudiced by Israel's "changing the facts" in Sharm el Sheikh, in Jerusalem, and on the West Bank. The passage of time may well tend to prejudice the Arab case. It may also, however, damage the Israeli position as well. The passage of time is not a zero-sum game in which losses for one party necessarily mean gains for the other. Time, by itself, does nothing to improve Israel's situation. The question is how Israel can best use time.

Although a reasonable Egyptian objective is to divide Israeli opinion, making it better politics for Prime Minister Meir or a successor to favor withdrawal from their territory, it does not follow that it is reasonable for Israel to support further divisions within Arab opinion. On the contrary, it would seem to Israel's interest to do what it can to strengthen the hands of those leaders capable of making peace with Israel. There is little danger of Israel's becoming too fragmented to be able to make effective political decisions. With today's divisions not only among the Palestinians but within the entire Arab world, there is a real risk of no one's being in a position to bring an end to Arab hostility toward Israel. With tact and good sense, Israel should be quietly doing what it can to strengthen Arab unity behind those leaders who can make peace with Israel.

There are many ways Israel can define its primary goal so far as the Arabs are concerned. Some define the goal in minimal terms, namely, that the Arabs should not destroy Israel. It seems better to try for more, with the hope both of achieving more and of enlisting the greater support that positive goals command over negative ones. I would suggest some such formulation as "to convert the Arabs from adversaries into friends."

Israel's goal is not to "win" a conflict with the Arabs, but to end it—to so act over a period of time that hostility is turned into friendship, without sacrificing basic values important to the people of Israel. As with those of other states, Israel's objectives of victory and peace are somewhat inconsistent. As with other states, the tendency is to place too much emphasis on short-term victories and not enough on establishing a long-term peaceful relationship.

In 1948 Israel would have been indeed content with the United Nations partition boundaries if the Arabs would have accepted Israel, accepted the partition, and lived in peace as good neighbors. At that time it was the demands of the Arabs which made such a peace impossible. Since then, the Arab states have come a long way. In accepting the Security Council resolution of November 1967 Egypt and Jordan have indicated a willingness to give Israel far more territory than the United Nations partition plan provided. Today if peace is beyond Israel's grasp it is in part because Israel (for whatever reasons) keeps it out of reach by asking for still more territory. As the Arabs have moved toward Israel's position on some issues, Israel has moved away.

It is not enough for Israel to justify its present policy by pointing to Arab hostility and Arab actions during the past twenty years. What Israel wants is to live in peace with friends. What Israel needs is an action program for doing that without incurring unreasonable risks.

Israel should not ask that a program be free from any risk. In this world there is no absolute security. Israel's present course of action involves substantial risks; any course of action will involve some.

Some Guidelines

The general guidelines of a course of action designed to convert Arab adversaries into friends of Israel should be publicly discussed and identified. The following comments are advanced to stimulate such consideration by you and by others.

1. Friendship Is a Process

Israel has fallen into the error, shared by the Arabs and perhaps United Nations mediators, among others, of tending to think that the alternative to the present kind of hostility is a big peace treaty that settles all the problems and draws a new map—a once-and-for-all solution. Both Israel and Egypt are thinking in terms of defining now, during the present period of distrust and hostility, the lines on that map and the terms of that solution. But this is like trying to draw up the terms of a marriage contract before any courting has taken place or the terms of a partnership agreement between people who distrust each other. If you want someone to be your spouse or your partner, you do not start off discussing the terms of the ultimate commitment. You start off with modest steps involving limited risks and limited commitment, and seek to develop a better relationship. Israel knows full well that confidence cannot be produced by a piece of paper. It should look for those bits of cooperation that not only give Egypt and other Arab states an opportunity to demonstrate that they are trustworthy but will also provide Israel wih a chance to establish its reasonableness and credibility with them.

Israel is understandably unwilling today to assume that its Arab neighbors will be friendly, and is certainly unwilling to take major military risks that rely on an Arab friendship that remains undemonstrated. Any map drawn by Israel during the present climate of distrust and hostility would almost certainly assure further distrust and further hostility. Wishing to eliminate any possible chance of a future military attack by Egypt, presently perceived as an enemy, Israel has been insisting that Egypt relinquish some of its territory to Israel and accept restrictions on the use of its own territory which Israel is unwilling to accept for itself. Asking Egypt to accept an inferior status based on the assumption of long-term enmity toward Israel is hardly designed to convince Egypt of Israel's friendship.

An alternative is to get started on the process of friendly relations. Israel should propose and take small steps designed to convince the Arabs of Israel's genuine friendship, steps that will advance the situation from one of conflict to one of cooperation, without major risks and without attempts to define today precise conditions for the long-term future.

2. Fractionate the Conflict

In a war situation all issues are seen as related to each other. The important question is not what is involved, but who. Trade depends not upon the price, but upon the nationality of the buyer. As long as "the other side" is involved, each issue is seen as leverage to be used in *the* conflict. In a peacetime situation, on the other hand, issues tend to be dealt with on their independent merits. The easier the working relationship between two countries —for example the United States and Canada—the less likely that one subject, such as fishing, will be seen as part of the same problem as another subject, such as tourism. It is not a matter of objective truth that some issues are related and others unrelated; it is a question of how people choose to treat them. If my neighbor wants to borrow ten dollars I may treat that as a wholly independent transaction, or I may say that I will lend him ten dollars if he will keep his dog off my lawn. Treating different matters separately is not only a reflection of better relations, it is a way of promoting them. One way for Israel to go about converting the present hostility into a better working relationship is for it to go forward on certain issues without insisting that they are related to others.

One way of breaking up issues is to break up the parties. Israel appreciates that "the Arabs" are by no means a single group that makes decisions as a unit. To insist that Israel will give no compensation to some Palestinian Arabs who abandoned property in Israel unless Iraq and Syria will give compensation to Jews who abandoned property in those countries would be to put "victory" on a small financial question ahead of improving the working relationship with Arab neighbors.

3. Be Forthcoming; Don't Hold All Points for Later Bargaining

Related to the notion of treating different subjects as separable is the idea of going forward on some matters without insisting upon an immediate and agreed quid pro quo. The conventional wisdom on international negotiations is that a state should be a "hard bargainer" that makes no "concessions" and that yields nothing to an opposing party except in exchange for something it wants that is equally or more valuable. To give such advice is to suggest that an international transaction is similar to one at a bazaar between strangers who have never seen each other before and will never do business again. All human experience suggests that where a continuing relationship is involved, there are far better ways to do business. Failing to insist upon a negotiated quid pro quo is not only a way of improving the relationship. It is frequently a way to get a better quid pro quo. In diplomacy as in the world of business, the bestowing of gifts need not be done with charity in mind.

A major part of Israel's task can be seen as that of courting a reluctant Arab. In such circumstances, for Israel to refuse to make any gift is to tie its own hands and to make success that much less likely. Israel is now free to make moves, such as permitting many more Palestinians to return to the West Bank, which might help Israel achieve its objective of converting adversaries into friends. For Israel to make its own action contingent upon action by some Arabs is to give those Arabs an effective veto over things which Israel can do to exert influence in pursuit of its own self-interest.

In the conventional wisdom of international affairs a state "loses" something by making a "concession"—a change of position from one that it has previously held to one favored by an adversary. If this were true, President Nixon would have lost by making his dramatic change of position with respect to the People's Republic of China. This "concession" was generally considered a political stroke that demonstrated strength, not weakness.

If Israel's objective is to convert Arabs from adversaries into friends, unilateral moves by Israel which help accomplish that objective are not "concessions" any more than spending money on a military airplane is a "concession." Each move should be examined for the actual cost involved, and for the possible favorable impact it may produce, free from any preconception that a unilateral move that appears to benefit one's adversary is either necessarily desirable or necessarily harmful.

4. Keep Flexible

A critical feature in the process of improving a relationship is the degree to which the views and interests of the other party are taken into account in developing one's own views. The closer and more friendly the relationship the more our final view as to what is desirable reflects not our independent judgment but rather a blending of views. To a remarkable extent Israel has publicly maintained an open view as to the future and as to what might be acceptable and what might not. This flexibility is highly desirable and should be continued. It might even be improved upon.

One way to combine the necessity of maintaining a bargaining position (which can be explained at home and abroad) with the desirability of being flexible is to state a present position but to indicate that it is subject to possible change. Another way to preserve flexibility is to advance alternative solutions.

The Israeli reply to Ambassador Jarring's letter of February 8, 1971, contained one sentence that struck many as indicating that Israel's position was unduly rigid, namely: "Israel will not withdraw to the pre–June 5, 1967, lines." This sentence was undoubtedly drafted in response to the kind of internal political situation that does not permit full attention to the problem of appearing flexible—and hence potentially friendly—to one's adversaries. In future circumstances such a point might be better put:

It is the present position of the government of Israel that the requirements of Israeli security will make it necessary to establish the Egyptian-Israeli boundary in a manner that departs from the pre–June 1967 boundary. Consequently, unless we are satisfied that the requirements of Israeli security can be otherwise met, or our position changes for other reasons, none of which we expect to happen, we do not anticipate that Israeli forces will withdraw to the June 4, 1967, line.

5. Talk to Influence Arabs, Not Spectators

Perhaps the most important guideline in trying to influence the Arabs is to think about *them*. Think of them as the audience for Israel's words and deeds. In the long run, it is Arabs with whom Israel must live, and it is they whom Israel wants to have as friendly neighbors.

Every government has to take into account the multiple audiences on whom its statements have an impact. Some Israeli statements are intended primarily for domestic consumption; some are intended to have their impact within the United States. But each is also overheard by the Arabs. On the front page of the daily paper Arab leaders read Israeli statements putting the worst possible construction on Arab positions. Arab statements accepting the existence of Israel are there dismissed by Israelis as insincere. Arab leaders overhear Israeli officials telling their public that Arabs are not to be trusted, that Egypt is now a Soviet puppet, that Israel has no intention of withdrawing from occupied territory, that not one Israeli soldier will withdraw until a formal treaty has been signed, and so forth.

Israel continues to ask for direct talks with Arabs, but talks to them comparatively infrequently by the many means available today. Foreign Minister Abba Eban on at least one occasion last year made a radio broadcast explicitly directed to Arab listeners. This apparently was a marked success, as one would expect where an able Israeli leader consciously thinks of himself as speaking to Arabs for the purpose of affecting what they think. Israel not only should make such radio appeals more often, but also should recognize Arabs as the primary audience for statements about the Arab-Israeli conflict. The Ministry of Foreign Affairs' excellent section for Arab matters should be asked to make sure that top officials are aware of Arab thinking and of Arab misperceptions of Israeli motives. The major task of the Israeli information program today is apparently seen as convincing Americans and other third parties of the merits of Israel and its position. The primary task should be to convince Arabs of those merits. The first step toward doing this is for Israel to think of itself as talking *to* Arabs for the purpose of convincing Arabs, not talking *about* Arabs for the purpose of convincing others.

Possible Elements of an Action Program Toward Egypt

Taking as its objective the conversion of Arab hostility into friendship and recognizing that this will take time, Israel should start without delay in designing some unilateral steps it might take in that direction. The best security for Israel is true friendship. Israel should work toward that security without in the meantime seriously undercutting its military defense capability. The following measures are illustrative of the kind of action that Israel should consider. These do not constitute a package or plan, but rather are individual elements that might be considered alternatively or cumulatively. They are not put forward as definitive drafts or suggestions but are rather intended to stimulate both the active consideration of an operational approach and the drafting of better steps.

1. Withdrawal of Civil Administration from the Sinai

Egyptians have two serious grievances over the continuing Israeli occupation of the Sinai. One is the fear of the loss of their sovereign territory. Although Israel professes to have no desire for territorial expansion, it is today building hotels at Sharm el Sheikh and extracting oil from the Sinai. To the Egyptians it looks as though Israel is occupying Egyptian territory for economic reasons and plans to keep it. The second grievance is the presence of Israeli troops on Egyptian territory, troops that have every intention of staying there unless and until other means are found to assure Israel that there is no significant risk of military attack.

An Israeli official suggested that one way of reassuring Egypt that it has nothing to fear from Israel, and at the same time assuring Israel that it has nothing to fear from Egypt, would be for Israel promptly to return all of the Sinai to Egyptian civil administration while retaining Israeli—and only Israeli—troops in the Sinai, pending future agreement or other developments.

Such a scheme has much to be said for it from the Israeli point of view. It leaves Israeli military forces in the Sinai at such places and in such numbers as Israel alone decides. It avoids all of the complexity and nuisance of international personnel. It protects Israel from the charge that it is expanding its sovereign territory under the pretext that all it seeks is military security. It relieves Egypt of much of the pressure for urgent action lest it permanently lose its territory. It provides a period of time in which Israelis and Egyptians might work together, with increasing confidence on both sides. It gives the Egyptians an opportunity to convince Israel that Egypt is in fact ready to live in peace with a Jewish state and that Israel can, over time, withdraw its military forces without risk. Finally, it can be seen as a form of staged withdrawal, consistent with the Security Council resolution. The plan would apparently provide no military threat to Israel's security since Israel could keep all of its military forces wherever it wanted to.

Ideally, under the proposal, Egyptian civilian officials would come into the Sinai and resume full responsibility for administering the civilian population of the perhaps fifty thousand people who are there. The Israeli military would keep a watch at the Canal to see that no Arab military units crossed into the Sinai, would have ground and air patrols over the Sinai, but could generally concentrate their forces into bases and limited zones so as to be all but invisible to the Arab population. The Israeli military would not constitute a military government, as at present. It would have no civil administration and no responsibility for the civil population unless, through guerrilla activity or otherwise, civilians began to constitute a military threat to Israel. Presumably a ranking Egyptian official or some other Egyptian liaison personnel would deal with a designated Israeli officer in order to minimize conflict or misunderstanding and work out problems that might come up.

The major difficulty in the proposal lies in making such cooperation politically acceptable to Egypt. It is too much to expect Egypt to take action that constitutes "agreement" to a plan under which Israeli troops will remain in the Sinai for an indefinite period. Yet without Egyptian participation Israel can hardly turn over civil administration of the Sinai. Against the wishes of Egypt, even local Arab self-government is probably unrealistic.

In these circumstances an Israeli move of this kind would have to be carefully designed so as to maximize its political acceptability in Egypt. It might well be desirable to involve some third party, like the United States or Britain, which could press the idea so that it would not look like "an Israeli trick." In any event it should be made abundantly clear that Arab resumption of civil jurisdiction over the Sinai would be wholly without prejudice to Egypt's position that the continued Israeli military presence is unauthorized and improper, and should be speedily terminated.

The following, in the form of a hypothetical statement made by the government of Israel, is a draft illustrating how this idea might be put into operational terms:

DRAFT 1
Israeli Withdrawal of Civil Administration from the Sinai

The following official statement was today approved by the Israeli Cabinet:

The government of Israel has long made clear that its only interest in the Sinai is one of military security. To put to rest fears that Israel is seeking to expand its sovereign territory into the Sinai for economic or other reasons Israel has today decided to restore all of the Sinai to Egyptian civil administration as rapidly as Egyptian officials are willing and able to assume it. This decision is made at the suggestion of the Big Four and as a first stage of the withdrawal contemplated in the Security Council resolution of November 22, 1967. While this decision is made unilaterally, it is contemplated that formal agreement will precede any subsequent withdrawal.

The withdrawal of civilian administration from the Sinai will take place subject to the following provisions:

a. Israel recognizes, effective immediately, that all of the Sinai beyond the boundary of June 4, 1967, with the exception of the Gaza Strip, is the sovereign territory of Egypt and subject to its civil jurisdiction. Israeli military government of this area will cease as soon as appropriate Egyptian officials indicate that they are ready and willing to assume responsibility for civil administration.

b. For the time being and pending agreement between Egypt and Israel with respect to the deployment of military forces within the Sinai, Egypt will continue to refrain from deploying any military personnel or military equipment east of the Suez Canal. Israeli military personnel remain for the time being under orders to prevent Egyptian soldiers or military equipment from crossing the Canal or the Gulf of Suez or otherwise being located in the Sinai.

    c. Israeli armed forces shall permit what they consider to be a reasonable number of Egyptian police equipped with side arms or other approved weapons to enter the Sinai for the purpose of maintaining law and order and controlling the civil population.

    d. All civil administration shall be the responsibility of Egypt. The government of Israel requests Egypt to deal fairly with persons and property that have come into the Sinai since June 1967. Failure to do so will make further withdrawal more difficult.

    e. The functions of all Israeli armed forces remaining in the Sinai shall be limited to the following:

    (1) to assure compliance with this decision,

    (2) to assure the security of Israel from attack, and

    (3) to assure the security of the forces themselves.

They shall be free to carry out these functions in such places and in such manner as the commanding officer of Israeli forces in the Sinai shall decide. He shall endeavor to see that these functions are carried out with a minimum of interference with and a minimum of impact on civilian activities within the Sinai.

    f. The commanding officer shall designate a liaison officer to whom Egyptian officials may make suggestions or complaints and who shall be available to work with Egyptian officials to minimize friction and to maximize cooperation.

    g. The government of Israel is committed to further withdrawal from the Sinai when and as this becomes consistent with Israeli security. Such withdrawal shall be carried out pursuant to agreement between Israel and Egypt. The time, manner, and extent of withdrawal shall be stipulated in that agreement.

    h. Action of Egypt or its officers in accepting civil responsibility in the Sinai or in cooperating with Israeli military personnel in any way is wholly without prejudice to the position of the

government of Egypt, and in particular is without prejudice to its
position that Israeli military personnel have no right to remain
in the Sinai.

I. Copies of this statement are being provided to the Secretary-
General. The Permanent Representative of Israel to the United
Nations will be available to meet with him or his special representative at any time to facilitate the implementation of this
decision or to resolve questions about it.

From the point of view of Israel, the main drawback to making
such a decision is that it makes less likely an establishment of
permanent total sovereignty over portions of the Sinai such as
Sharm el Sheikh. But Israel is more interested in security than in
territorial expansion. Such a decision would appear to promote
Israeli security in two ways. Security through military defense
would not be reduced. Israeli military forces could remain in the
Sinai with the same freedom of action as they have at present.
Security through political friendship would be promoted. Israel
would be taking action that should both reduce Egyptian fears of
loss of territory and provide a situation in which Egyptians, like
Arabs on the West Bank, can develop a realistic knowledge of
Israel and Israelis through practical cooperative experience.

When I asked the Israeli who first suggested this idea to me
how long he would expect Israeli military forces to remain in the
Sinai under such an arrangement, he offered a simple standard.
"When Golda Meir can go shopping in Cairo and I can visit the
Pyramids, and neither of us will have to worry, then the troops
can be withdrawn." I can think of no way in which Israel might
hasten that day at less risk to itself than by taking a step along the
lines proposed.

2. Unilateral Withdrawal to a Mid-Sinai Line

An alternative form of withdrawal that Israel might undertake
unilaterally is the removal of its military forces from more than
half the Sinai by moving the Israeli forward position from the

eastern bank of the Suez Canal to a line that would leave Israel in control of Sharm el Sheikh, a band of territory along the Gulf of Aqaba, and the northeastern portion of the Sinai between Gaza and El Arish. This would leave Israel in military control of that portion of the Sinai which Prime Minister Meir suggested in a press interview Israel would like to retain in a final settlement for reasons of military security. The difference is that rather than wait for a negotiated settlement, Israel could act immediately. This proposal was suggested to me by an American Jew who thought that Israel should take a major dramatic step both to regain domestic and international support and to move the Middle East toward peace.

Rather than quarrel over the Suez Canal and the number and character of military men and equipment that Egypt should bring across the Canal into the Sinai, Israel could provide an occasion for the Egyptians to demonstrate their peaceful intentions, and at the same time provide for itself a chance to test those intentions. Any decision about further withdrawal would be made in the light of knowledge as to what Egypt had done with respect to Israeli shipping through the Suez Canal and with respect to Egyptian military forces in the Sinai.

Since the new line would reflect Israel's own idea of a secure boundary, the military risk in withdrawing to it should not be excessive. The major danger with such a move would be that Egypt would flunk the Israeli-created test as to its intentions. In catering to domestic opinion, Egypt might well rush large military forces across the Suez Canal and announce that only after Israel had withdrawn all of its forces from all of the Sinai would any Israeli ships be allowed through the Canal. Israel would then be convinced that Egypt remained bellicose and that no further withdrawal was possible. A hostile and stalemated confrontation might then be expected along the new Israeli line, with Israel in a somewhat worse position militarily than at present.

The objective is not, however, to create a test of Egyptian intentions for Egypt to fail, but rather to affect those intentions for the better. Substantial advance discussion through Ambassador Jarring or through the United States would appear desirable in order to make certain that Egypt understands what is expected of it, and that there is a good chance of its conduct being sufficiently peaceful and cooperative to pave the way for further cooperation. In effect, Israel might want to negotiate the text of its unilateral move.

As a basis for such advance discussions, Israel might consider sending a letter to the United States, for example, along the following lines:

DRAFT 2

Israeli Letter Exploring the Idea of
Unilateral Partial Withdrawal

The Honorable William P. Rogers
Secretary of State
Washington, D.C.
Dear Mr. Secretary:

Despite your energetic and persistent efforts it has so far proved impossible to reach an interim agreement between Israel and Egypt providing for a partial withdrawal of Israeli armed forces from the Suez Canal and the opening of the Canal, together with reasonable restrictions on Egyptian military activity east of the Canal. We are reluctant, however, to let the matter drop. If we are to convert the present period of hostility and distrust between Israel and Egypt into one of friendship, steps must be taken that permit each side to put its best foot forward and to demonstrate to the other its peaceful intentions and its willingness to exercise self-restraint in the interest of peace and justice in the Middle East.

Although we do not agree with it, we understand the reluctance of Egypt to make a formal commitment never to use military force against Israel at a time when we are holding Egyptian territory by military force and when peaceful methods have so

far failed to produce peace. We can also understand the reluctance of Egypt in an interim agreement to accept formal
restrictions on the stationing of Egyptian troops on Egyptian
territory east of the Suez Canal. We trust that the Egyptians, in
turn, can understand our reluctance to move a line of imminent
battle closer to the population centers of Israel. If Egypt is going
to wage war against Israel, we would obviously prefer the battle
to be on Arab territory and as far from Tel Aviv and Jerusalem
as possible.

In these circumstances we are looking for a way to move toward
withdrawal and peace without a formal agreement. It has been
suggested to us that the government of Israel should take a
unilateral step of partial withdrawal to provide Egypt with an
occasion on which it could demonstrate its good faith and its
interests in peace by exercising self-restraint. In particular, it has
been suggested that Israel announce a decision along the following lines:

    a. The government of Israel today announced that during the
       next sixty days it will withdraw all of its armed forces from
       the east bank of the Suez Canal so that all of its military
       personnel in the Sinai will be east of a line defined as
       follows: . . . .

    b. This major move is taken to demonstrate the Israeli desire
       for peace and to create circumstances in which Egypt may
       similarly take unilateral measures to convince the people
       of Israel of Egypt's good faith and peaceful intentions.

    c. No formal conditions have been exacted nor have any
       promises been received from Egypt or others in exchange
       for this measure of withdrawal. Nevertheless, it should be
       made exceedingly clear that the willingness of the govern-
       ment of Israel to undertake further measures of with-
       drawal will be affected by the words and deeds of Egypt.

If Egypt should refrain from moving any significant number of military men across the Canal, should open the Suez Canal on a nondiscriminatory basis to ships of all nations, should maintain the cease-fire, and should by other means demonstrate that Egypt poses no military threat to Israel, then we foresee no difficulty in undertaking additional measures of withdrawal, preferably through agreement. If, on the other hand, Egypt should move large numbers of troops into the Sinai with no apparent purpose other than to attack Israeli forces, if it should open the Suez Canal for the ships of some nations but not for Israeli ships, and if it should otherwise demonstrate by word and deed that Israel has reason to fear a military attack from Egypt, then we anticipate great difficulty in arranging for any further withdrawal of Israeli forces that would simply place them in an even less advantageous position from which to defend themselves against such attack.

A serious argument against Israel's considering any such unilateral withdrawal lies in the substantial risk that, rather than promote a peaceful settlement, this step might make such a settlement less likely. If such a move by Israel were met with conduct on the part of Egypt that the people of Israel regarded as bellicose, aggressive, and unjustified—if the response to our generous deed were a slap in the face—the chance for any kind of peaceful settlement in the foreseeable future would be much worse, not better.

Before giving further consideration to this proposed uni-lateral step we would be interested in your judgment as to whether or not it would be constructive. In particular, we would welcome your judgment as to whether Israel could expect the kind of response for which we would be hoping. We would also welcome any suggestions you might have as to how the language announcing any such decision might be improved to make a favorable reaction by Egypt more likely. We assume that in forming your judgment and suggestions you will wish to discuss this matter with officials of Egypt, and, of course, we have no objection to your doing so.

We look forward to hearing from you.

Sincerely yours,

_____

(Government of Israel)

Such an initiative by Israel might go far to change the climate of the current conflict and to provide an opportunity for peace to break out.

3. A Sample Withdrawal

A smaller step with which Israel might begin the process of trying to convert Egyptian hostility into friendship would be to offer the unilateral withdrawal of Israeli personnel and equipment from a designated zone of the Sinai somewhere along the Gulf of Suez. Preferably it would be some place that had had a small Arab community such as a fishing village. The move would constitute a gesture but it might also provide an opportunity for some on-the-ground cooperation between Egyptian and Israeli military officers. It would also provide, at little risk, information of use in planning and considering further measures of withdrawal. It would provide the Egyptians with a chance to demonstrate that they can resume control over a portion of the Sinai without creating a military threat to Israel. Such an offer might be made through Ambassador Jarring and might run along the following lines:

DRAFT 3
Israeli Letter Proposing Sample Withdrawal

His Excellency, Dr. Gunnar Jarring
Special Representative of the Secretary-General
United Nations
New York, New York
Dear Mr. Ambassador:

In order to move forward toward peace and to develop a better understanding of the difficulties that may be involved in the staged withdrawal of Israeli armed forces from their present positions to secure and recognized boundaries, the government of Israel has decided to withdraw its forces, permanently, from a small designated portion of the Sinai bordering on the Gulf of Suez. This withdrawal is contingent upon nothing other than the expressed willingness of Egypt to accept responsibility for what takes place within the area from which our forces have been withdrawn.

We hope that this small step will provide an occasion for military officers on both sides to learn how a change in a military line can best take place peacefully and without misunderstanding and without use or threats of force. We also hope that the response of Egypt to this step will be such as to encourage the government of Israel to believe that large-scale withdrawal of its forces can take place without in any way increasing a military threat to Israel or to its armed forces.

This trial withdrawal will take place within thirty days of your communicating to us the expressed willingness of Egypt to accept responsibility for what takes place within the area from which our forces will be withdrawn. Such expression on their part is, of course, wholly without prejudice to Egypt's position that Israeli forces have no rights whatever within the Sinai.

The area from which withdrawal will take place is defined as follows: . . . .

Sincerely yours,

(Government of Israel)

Possible Elements of an Action Program Toward the Palestinians

Perhaps even more important than Israel's taking steps designed to influence Egypt directly is Israel's moving forward with respect to the Palestinians. For many years this could be thought of simply as a refugee problem. Today in addition to the humanitarian problem of more than a million refugees there is the political problem of Palestinian self-determination. The Arabs who lived in Palestine—within the mandated territory that covers what is now Israel, the West Bank, and Gaza—have developed a political consciousness that must be dealt with. It is to Israel's interest to turn these Arabs, as well as the Egyptians, into friends. And dealing with Palestinians is not only an end in itself. Egypt is committed to justice for the Palestinians. If nothing is being done about the Palestinians it will be politically costly to Cairo's position in the Arab world for Cairo to become more friendly toward Israel. For Israel to deal with the Palestinians will make it easier for Egypt to deal with Israel.

The physical humanitarian problem of finding places to live and jobs for the Palestinians is not a task of enormous magnitude. The world could now find room for them outside of Palestine just as the world before 1948 could have found room for the Jewish refugees outside of Palestine. The same kind of feelings that cause many Israelis to want their own homeland in a particular place cause many Palestinians to want their own homeland in the same place. Understanding Palestinian feelings rather than denying them will help Israel convert Palestinian Arabs into good neighbors and good citizens.

There are three aspects of the Palestinian problem:

1. The humanitarian problem. It is to Israel's interest to get as many Palestinians as possible out of the camps and into homes and regular jobs where they are likely to become more affirmatively involved in their own future and less negatively involved in Israel's future.

2. The political problem. The sense of political injustice should be dealt with. However reasonable they seem to Israelis, the discriminatory consequences of Israeli immigration policy strike many Palestinians as outrageous. A Jew from South Africa or South America who has never seen the Middle East has a legal right to go "home" to Israel, while an Arab who lived there for generations may not return to his own lands for one reason only—he is not a Jew. The Arabs who left Israel in 1948 and the Arabs who left the West Bank in 1967, whatever the mixture of motives that caused them to flee, were not voluntarily abandoning their homes for good. Whatever may make sense now should not be justified on the basis of such a myth.

3. The problem of Palestinian participation. Palestinians should be involved in working out their peaceful future with Israel. Whatever the future, it will set better with Palestinians if their leaders are deeply involved in developing it. And it will be easier for Palestinians to compromise their own claims than it will be for other Arabs to do so for them.

1. A Further Stage of a Refugee Return Program

Rather than making promises of generosity in the future— promises that are heavily discounted in the Arab world—perhaps Israel should build on the "open bridges" policy already launched so successfully.

It is difficult for Palestinians to accept a fixed quota that would formally preclude the right to return of some of those who lived in what is now Israel. There is an interesting parallel between the Jewish and the Arab insistence on this *right* to return. Israel insists that every Jew anywhere in the world must have the right to "return" to Israel. When Arabs express concern over the consequences of such massive immigration (which they fear would lead to Israeli expansion) they are told not to worry, that although every Jew has a right to immigrate, as a practical matter only a limited number will. This prediction fails to reassure the Arabs.

On the other side, Palestinians usually insist that every Palestinian anywhere in the world—and his family—should have a right to return to what was Palestine, and that all those who lived in what has become Israel must have the right to return there. When Israelis express concern over the consequences of such massive immigration (which they fear would drastically alter the Jewish character of Israel) they may be told not to worry, that although every Palestinian must have the right to return, as a practical matter only a limited number will. This prediction is equally unsuccessful in reassuring Israelis.

In order to move forward it will probably be necessary to act in a manner neither affirming nor denying the right of all Palestinians to return.

It will not be easy either for Palestinian leadership or for Israel to accept a practical solution to the refugee problem without both sides having more knowledge of what the practical problem is. If it were possible to develop a sound basis for concluding how many refugees would in fact choose each of the various options offered, it might be possible to reach an agreement in terms of numbers or rights. Arabs might agree to a numerical ceiling, knowing that that ceiling was large enough to permit all those who actually wanted to return to Israel to do so. Israel might accept the principle that certain categories of Palestinians had a right to return to Israel, knowing that not too many would actually come. Or Israel might concede that Arabs who formerly lived in what has become Israel could have the same right to return as do Jews under the Law of Return, namely, the right to come to Israel and also the right to settle in Israel

. . . unless the Minister of Immigration is satisfied that the applicant (1) is engaged in an activity directed against the Jewish

people; or (2) is likely to endanger public health or the security
of the State.

A decision to amend the Law of Return to make it applicable to
Arabs who were formerly resident in what is now Israel would
presumably require the conclusion that the application of the security exception would not take place so often as to create a political backlash.

Taking a census among the refugee camps and elsewhere
would be an unreliable method of ascertaining the desires of individual Palestinians. Those whose views were solicited would
have little idea of what they were really choosing, and would be
subject to political exhortation. The results of any such question-
naire might have no relationship to what people faced with a real
choice sometime later would actually choose.

To meet these problems, it is suggested that Israel design and
execute a "sample" program in which several thousand Arabs
who left Israel are given an opportunity to make and carry out an
informed choice among several fair options that are offered to
them. The following draft illustrates the kind of announcement
that Israel might make:

DRAFT 4

Israeli Announcement of a Pilot Refugee Program

The government of Israel today announced that it is inaugurat-
ing discussions with the United Nations Relief and Works Agency,
seeking its cooperation and assistance in implementing a new
program under which up to ten thousand Arabs formerly resident
in Israel would be given an opportunity during the next ten months
to return to Israel.

The new program will involve presenting applicants with real
choices. The government of Israel emphasized that at the present
time it is making no commitment as to the total number of Arab
refugees who will be permitted to settle in Israel and that the

figure of ten thousand is not the total number of those to be offered a choice but simply the size of this pilot program. Further resettlement and repatriation programs will be undertaken in light of the information developed through this program.

All Arabs who were formerly permanent residents within that portion of the Palestine mandate that falls within the boundaries of Israel as of 1949–1967 may apply for the pilot program. Priority will be given to those who actually resided in the area (as contrasted with relatives of former residents), and among former residents it is intended to give priority to those who lived there for the longest period of time.

Persons accepted for the program will be offered four choices:

1. Return to Israel. In most cases the intervening period of more than twenty years will make it impossible to offer the same house or lot as may have constituted the former residence, but each accepted applicant will be offered a specific location, with terms and circumstances clearly defined. Those returning to Israel must be willing to live in peace as Israeli citizens. Like other Israeli citizens they may, of course, seek to bring about changes within Israel through peaceful political methods as permitted by law.

2. Settle in the West Bank. Many of the "old" refugees who left Israel in 1948 lived near Jericho or elsewhere in the West Bank for almost twenty years. Each accepted applicant will be offered an opportunity to settle on the West Bank in lieu of returning to Israel. Again, it is contemplated that each person will be offered a specific location under defined terms.

3. Accept a resettlement allowance. Accepted applicants who would prefer to settle permanently elsewhere than in Israel or the West Bank and who have obtained the necessary permission from the state concerned to do so will be offered a cash re-

settlement allowance in lieu of all other rights and claims against Israel. This will be a specific amount based upon circumstances and determined according to guidelines to be developed in consultation with the United Nations Relief and Works Agency.

4. Wait and see. Each accepted applicant will also have the option of rejecting the first three choices and awaiting whatever the future may bring, without receiving any commitment from Israel and without waiving any rights or claims that he may have.

It is proposed that arrangements be made for applicants whose papers have been processed and who have been accepted for the pilot program to make a several days' visit to both Israel and the West Bank before making a final decision.

The government of Israel recognizes that this pilot program falls short of being a solution to the refugee problem or to the political aspirations of Palestinian Arabs. But it is not within the power of Israel acting by itself to produce such a solution. Not only will this pilot program, if successful, facilitate the settlement of Arab refugees at places of their choice at the rate of one thousand per month, it will also provide the kind of solid information about their real preferences, and about ways of determining and satisfying them, that should help all the countries of the world to provide the resources and the opportunities needed to resolve this situation to the best interests of all concerned.

Israel is reluctant to admit that persons who never accepted Israeli citizenship have rights to come to Israel other than as defined by Israeli law. To concede that Arab refugees have some superior legal rights antedating the state of Israel seems to throw into question the legitimacy or the completeness of Israel's statehood. Israel insists that, being a sovereign state, it alone should decide the question of who should be allowed to immigrate. And yet Israel's current position apparently is to postpone any decision about which refugees should be allowed to return to Israel and which should not until that decision can be jointly reached with others through negotiation.

Since Israel, despite its current desire for negotiations, nonetheless maintains that the question of immigration is basically one for unilateral decision, it would seem wiser for Israel to start dealing with at least part of the refugee problem unilaterally. The more that Israel demonstrates that it is capable of dealing fairly with this question on its own, the more its rights to do so will be respected. Such respect is important if there is ever to be a sense of finality to a resolution of the refugee problem. For whatever doubts might be cast upon Israel's legal right to decide which Arab refugees can return to Israel and which cannot, even greater doubts can be cast upon the legal right of any other state or individual to waive the right of some Palestinian to return to his native home, assuming he has such a right. It would be extremely hard for any Arab state or leader to say that he had the legal power to extinguish the rights of the Palestinians. Rather than look forward to some future "binding" international agreement to terminate rights that Israel says are exclusively a matter of domestic law, Israel would seem well advised to start treating those rights as a matter of domestic law, and to do it so fairly that the countries of the world—including the Arab states—respect Israel's decisions. Israel should not wait for negotiations and then argue that immigration questions are nonnegotiable—that they are for Israel alone to decide. One way to start is along the lines of the above pilot proposal.

2. Allow West Bank Refugees to Return

Whether or not additional Arabs are now allowed to settle in Israel as Israeli citizens, more can be done in the immediate future with respect to allowing the 1967 refugees from the West Bank to return and settle on the West Bank.

Israel has already been willing to let many West Bank refugees return to the West Bank, particularly relatives of those permanently living there. A policy of returning "West Bankers" to the

West Bank would seem to be clearly in the interest of Israel. One can safely say that the Palestinians living constructive lives on the West Bank are by and large more realistic about Israel and more willing to live in peace with Israel than are the Palestinians living in refugee camps outside of Amman.

There is a risk, of course, that some guerrillas would enter despite a screening process. But there is certainly less enthusiasm for terrorist activities on the West Bank than among those in the camps, and it is probably easier for Israeli intelligence to deal with those on the West Bank than with those in Jordan.

Major areas of concern are logistical and economic, including such questions as how rapidly Palestinians could be brought back to the West Bank, how rapidly the economy could support them, how rapidly new housing and other necessary construction could take place, and how the funds would be raised. In offering refugees a chance to settle on the West Bank, Israel should probably extend the offer not only to former residents but also to those who had lived elsewhere in the Palestine mandate, including Gaza and what has become Israel. A rapid and booming program of settling Palestinians on the West Bank might solve much of the problem of those who claim rights to return to Israel. Many might prefer a bird in the hand, and accept permanent settlement on the West Bank, rather than take their chances on the possibility of later being allowed—and wanting—to return and live as Israeli citizens in Israel.

In expanding the open bridges policy to the point of permitting essentially all Palestinian refugees who want to do so to settle on the West Bank as soon as possible, Israel should call on the international community for financial, and perhaps administrative, assistance. One way to do so would be to call on the World Bank. Israel might consider writing the bank a letter along the following lines:

DRAFT 5
Israeli Letter to World Bank on West Bank Development Project

President
International Bank for Reconstruction and Development
1818 H Street, N.W.
Washington, D.C.
Dear Sir:

You are aware of the difficulties that have impeded progress toward a comprehensive settlement of the Arab-Israeli conflict in the Middle East. One tragedy of this delay is the fact that thousands upon thousands of Palestinian Arabs remain in limbo. The government of Israel has decided that it should do something to alleviate this situation and to move forward with a program for settling at least some Palestinians on the West Bank in permanent homes even in the absence of the resolution of other questions, and even if the settlement of some refugees will not solve the problem of others. We would like the advice and assistance of the World Bank in developing and implementing this program.

The government of Israel believes that this West Bank program could be based on the following principles:

1. Every Palestinian Arab who is prepared to pursue his future through peaceful political means should be allowed to return to make his home somewhere within the territory of the former mandate of Palestine.

2. All Arabs formerly resident on the West Bank should be allowed as rapidly as possible to return to their homes on the West Bank or, if that is not feasible, to new homes on the West Bank.

3. Other Palestinian refugees, wherever their original home may have been, who would like to settle permanently on the West Bank should be permitted to do so as soon as housing and other necessary facilities can be provided.

4. The international community should contribute substantially to the financial costs of providing the housing, new towns, and other facilities necessary to assure the returning refugees of a viable economic existence. The government of Israel itself is prepared to assist in meeting these financial costs.

5. Palestinian Arabs who will be settling on the West Bank should be involved in the designing and implementation of the West Bank development project.

6. Palestinians who prefer to wait and see what other opportunities the future may offer should be permitted to do so.

In moving forward to permit this major extension of the open bridges policy, the government of Israel is not foreclosing the possibility that a significant number of Arabs who wish to return to Israel and to live in peace as Israeli citizens may later be permitted to do so. That is a more difficult question and one that should be easier to resolve in the light of experience with the West Bank project.

The development and implementation of this project will obviously require close collaboration among many different parties. We hope that the World Bank will be willing to play an active role in bringing together the views, the expertise, the resources, and the individuals most likely to make such a project a success. Although the government of Israel, as the government currently exercising jurisdiction over the West Bank, must retain a final say over security and other matters, as many decisions as possible should be taken by others and particularly by those whose homes and futures are directly involved.

The government of Israel plans to move forward immediately,
to permit former residents of the West Bank who have homes
available to them to return as rapidly as possible, consistent
with Israel's being satisfied that they intend to live peacefully.
We would like the Bank to begin immediately in working with us
and others to permit an orderly and rapid return of Palestinians
to the West Bank. Even at a rate of one thousand per week it
would take almost ten years to settle half a million.

After you have had a chance to consider this letter we hope
you will be in touch with our ambassador in Washington.

Sincerely yours,

_____

(Government of Israel)

There are a number of other ways in which Israel could move
to increase the rate of return to the West Bank of Arab refugees.
The fact that nobody is pressing Israel to do so is hardly a reason
for failing to do so.

3. Make It Politically Easy for Palestinians to Talk Directly

It is obviously to Israel's interest that Palestinian Arabs who are
dissatisfied with the present situation have peaceful avenues
through which to express themselves. If the only way they can
express themselves is through hand grenades or other guerrilla
activity, such activity becomes more likely. And the longer the
hostile activity remains the basic means of communication with
Israel, the more difficult it will be for Israel to convert hostility
into friendship.

Although Palestinians are at the heart of the conflict, they have
not in this century had a hand in shaping the political arrangements defining their own destiny. That a durable peace can be
reached in the area while many Palestinians continue to harbor
deep and legitimate grievances seems unlikely. The Jordanian
army has "clipped the wings" of the commandos, and the Pales-

tinian military capability is certainly not great enough for the Palestinians physically to prevent a solution's being reached. Nevertheless, the Palestinians probably have a "spoiler capacity" through the impact within Israel of an articulate Palestinian threat. Would an Israeli cabinet be politically able to accept withdrawal from the West Bank to an agreed boundary if Palestinian spokesmen, instead of promising peace, were threatening to continue from more advanced positions a campaign of terrorism and sabotage? The military effectiveness of such a campaign is less significant than the powerful political shadow it would cast.

Israel is correct in insisting that it cannot now "negotiate" with Palestinians. There is no Palestinian in a position to speak with authority for the diverse organizations, individuals, and views that today constitute "the Palestinians." Further, the political structure of the situation apparently precludes any Palestinian's sitting down with Israel and advancing a "Palestinian position" and remaining the next day an accepted spokesman for the Palestinians. Both Egypt and Israel find that to advance a reasonable position indicating some willingness to compromise is to incur immediate domestic political costs with no offsetting international rewards. The same phenomenon is much more true for a Palestinian spokesman since there is even less agreement on the kind of future Palestinians want. There is no possible statement concerning the preferred future that would not subject the spokesman to severe criticism either from the Palestinians in the refugee camps, from those supporting the commando movement, from those supporting King Hussein, or from those on the West Bank—or perhaps from all of them.

Officials from Israel have sometimes indicated a willingness to sit down with Palestinians, particularly those now in Jerusalem or elsewhere on the West Bank, but have usually insisted that the Palestinians "represent somebody." One can blame the Palestinian movement for not getting its own house in order, but it is to Israel's interest to "domesticate" Palestinian forms of expression, whether or not Palestinian views can be effectively represented by some authorized spokesman.

In these circumstances, it would seem desirable for Israel to solicit and to welcome advice from Palestinian individuals and organizations whether or not they can legitimately speak for and commit a large number of other Palestinians. In the absence of formal representation, informal participation is better than none. Rather than ask, Who are the Palestinians? Israel should do the best it can to make it easy for Palestinians to participate peacefully in determining the future of Gaza, the West Bank, and the Arab interests in Jerusalem. And rather than ask that some designated Palestinians be spokesmen for Palestinian views on all issues, it might be better, as a way of increasing direct discussions, to ask Palestinians to help resolve particular substantive problems. Such an approach is illustrated in the following draft of an Israeli letter:

DRAFT 6
Israeli Letter Asking Advice of a Leading West Bank Palestinian

Dear Mr. _____:

The government of Israel is contemplating soliciting international financial support for development schemes on the West Bank to advance the economy of the area and to facilitate a prompt return to the West Bank of Arab refugees who formerly lived there and who wish to return. At the formative stages of this project and before making any commitments or public announcements we would be interested in receiving advice and suggestions from those for whom the development would be taking place and those most affected by it.

We understand fully the impossibility under the present circumstances of any Palestinian purporting to make commitments on behalf of other Palestinians. On the other hand, however much you may disagree with the continuing military occupation of the West Bank today, we trust that you will recognize the propriety of our trying to learn Arab views about the long-lasting development for Arabs of Arab land that presumably someday will be free of that occupation.

At this stage we would like to invite you and half a dozen other distinguished Palestinians to a preliminary meeting that will be held in my office on the twenty-fourth of this month at 10:00 A.M. Others being invited (and receiving letters identical to this one) are . . . .

At the preliminary meeting we will outline our tentative thinking on West Bank resettlement and development and will welcome any preliminary reactions you might care to offer. We would also hope to receive your ideas about the process of consultation and solicitation of Palestinian views. In particular we would welcome any suggestions you might have of additional Palestinians who might be invited to subsequent meetings to discuss the proposal. At subsequent meetings we would hope to receive more detailed comments and reactions based upon your further reflection and any discussions you may have had with others.

Let me assure you that our interest is in seeing that any development project that goes forward is informed by the best thinking of those who will be affected by it. At no time will you be asked to "approve" a project or to commit yourself or others. Your willingness to give us advice is wholly without prejudice to your position on any matter.

For the time being, in view of the tentative nature of our thinking, we contemplate no publicity about this project or about our seeking Arab views with respect to it. Should it become necessary to do so, we would release the text of these identical letters of invitation.

I look forward to seeing you on the twenty-fourth. Please let my office know if you will be able to attend.

Sincerely yours,

_____

(Government of Israel)

4. Make It Easier for Palestinians at the United Nations

Palestinians feel that they were left out of the Security Council resolution of November 22, 1967. The Security Council did affirm the necessity of "achieving a just settlement of the refugee problem"; but the resolution did not treat the refugees as Palestinians with political aspirations. Further, by referring only to contacts with "states," the resolution did not include Palestinians among those with whom Ambassador Jarring was supposed to talk. Yet Palestinian voices ought to be heard in United Nations consideration of the Middle East.

Israeli sponsorship of Palestinian participation in the implementation of Security Council Resolution 242 would probably be the kiss of death so far as Palestinian willingness to participate is concerned. But Israel should certainly refrain from creating obstacles to Palestinian participation. At the most, it might privately indicate in advance that it would have no objections to such participation if it could be worked out.

Possible Element of an Action Program Toward Jordan

Israel is interested in converting into friendship not only Egyptian and Palestinian hostility, but also Jordanian hostility. The fact that King Hussein seems less hostile to Israel than do either Egyptian or Palestinian leaders is not a reason for ignoring Jordan. Indeed, it may well be a reason to be particularly vigorous in pursuing an interim agreement with Jordan. Some progress toward peace may be easier to attain with Jordan than with others and, once obtained, may be contagious.

1. Offer an Interim Agreement

There is a wide variety of possible interim agreements covering the West Bank and Gaza. The essential dilemma is apparent. Israel cannot reasonably be expected to withdraw its military forces or even to relinquish its military government of the area unless and until it knows who is going to assume civil administration of that area. Israel will not want to turn over the West Bank permanently to Jordan or anybody else against the wishes of the local population. There is no way effectively to determine the wishes of the local population so long as they remain under Israeli military rule, since any decision reached under exclusive Israeli authority is subject to challenge by disgruntled Arabs.

What is needed with respect to the West Bank is some preliminary political activity that will structure the situation so that local residents will be able with demonstrable fairness to make decisions about their future. As suggested above, some direct Palestinian participation would appear desirable. Yet most observers conclude that the West Bank should not be split from the East Bank, and that Jordan and the West Bank should have some continuing intimate relationship, presumably as parts of the same state. Certainly Israel should not appear to exclude Jordan from consideration about the West Bank.

Perhaps the best way to start active consideration of some form of interim agreement with Jordan with respect to the West Bank is to ask the United States or Ambassador Jarring or his successor to see if they might lend a hand. The following draft suggests one approach:

DRAFT 7
Israeli Letter Suggesting an Interim Agreement with Jordan

Dear _____:

You are familiar with both the efforts and the difficulties in trying to establish a constructive interim agreement between Israel and Egypt. Despite the difficulties, we believe that the effort is sound and that steps should also be taken toward reaching an interim agreement between Israel and Jordan.

With respect to the West Bank and Gaza it is even more obvious that some interim measures must be undertaken before a final settlement of boundary and security questions can be agreed upon. For example, there is today no one in the world who claims—let alone is generally recognized to have—legal authority to make a binding commitment on behalf of the people or territory of Gaza. Similarly, both Israel and Jordan have recognized that the Arab occupants of the West Bank should have some voice in determining the final terms of their future, yet today there is no clear picture as to how or when that process ought to take place.

In these circumstances we believe that discussions involving Israel and Jordan should be initiated on the question of how to proceed with respect to the West Bank and perhaps Gaza, and perhaps with respect to other issues as well. The purpose of the discussions would be to reach an interim agreement covering measures to be undertaken in the immediate future. Certainly, Israel and Jordan will not reach the peace so urgently desired by the people of the area unless some agreed steps are taken in that direction within the months immediately ahead.

We would like to invite your assistance in this effort.

Sincerely yours,

_____

(Government of Israel)

This has been a long letter, even longer than I had anticipated when I started to write it. Much of it will appear obvious to you, and some, perhaps, will be uncongenial to your thinking. If I am correct your reaction to many of these suggestions will be that they are "unrealistic"—that they do not take into account the realities of domestic Israeli public opinion. As I said at the outset, none of the suggestions is advanced as "the" answer. They are designed to stimulate a recognition that the central job for Israel over the months and years ahead is to influence *Arab* thinking. They are also designed to stimulate work on specific, operational moves that

Israel might take at minimal risk to its security in order to convince Arab leaders and Arab public opinion of Israel's integrity, good intentions, and credibility. My hope is that you and your colleagues with your greater knowledge and familiarity with the facts will be able to improve on these ideas and, indeed, develop better ones.

With the thought that this letter contains ideas of possible interest to a wider audience, I am planning to publish it (with your name omitted) together with comparable letters that I have written to others involved in the Middle East problem. If you have any reactions, criticisms, or comments I would obviously welcome them. Needless to say, there is no implication that you or anyone else agrees—or disagrees—with anything that I have written.

I have not forgotten your comments about the necessity of candor by any third party who hopes to play a constructive role through discussions with various parties in a conflict. I am sending you copies of the letters that I have written to others, giving them the same kind of advice from their point of view that this letter tries to give you from yours. I am also sending a copy of this letter to them. At least I will have met your standard of full disclosure.

With warm personal regards,

ROGER FISHER

4.
Letter to a Palestinian

August 22, 1971

Dear ———— [a member of the executive committee of the
Palestine Liberation Organization],

I was sorry to miss you at the meeting of the Palestine National
Council in Cairo in July. There were some loose ends following
our January discussion in Amman which should have been tied up.
Let me try to clear the air by setting down once more the general
approach that I think the Palestine Liberation Organization ought
to be pursuing and by suggesting some specific illustrations of how
that might be done.

Ends and Means

Palestinians have a right to select their own ultimate goal. The
ultimate Palestinian goal, as I understand it, is a secular state of
Palestine, in which Christians, Moslems, and Jews live with equal
rights. It is unclear whether this concept of a future Palestine includes the territory and people of Jordan, but it certainly includes
the territory of Israel, Gaza, and the West Bank. There has also
been some discussion as to whether the only Jews who would be
allowed to remain would be those who had reached Palestine prior
to a certain date. I understand the current concept to be that all
Jews willing to live in peace in a secular state could remain and
that future immigration would be on a nondiscriminatory basis. If

I have any expertise it is not in goal picking—not in substituting my values for yours—but rather in stimulating you to think through how you might best move forward toward your goal. But some comments about goals might be in order.

Palestinians should not assume that because they have a moral or a legal right to something, it is the best goal for them to seek. It might be, for instance, that as a consequence of what has happened during the past twenty-three years Palestinians would in fact be happier in an Arab state of their own than in a state with a large Jewish population. A second comment is that in selecting an ultimate goal that will be difficult to attain and might be a long way off under the best of circumstances, it is desirable to identify some intermediate goals. If my young son wants to be a United States senator, fine. That is his goal. But he would be well advised to adopt some intermediate goals along the way. To adopt an intermediate goal is not inconsistent with having a quite different ultimate goal. In fact intermediate goals are usually indispensable in attaining a difficult long-range objective.

As I see the situation, the tragedies of the past and the magnitude of present grievances are tending to divert Palestinians from realistic, practical discussion of what ought to happen next and how Palestinian leadership can make those results more likely. Those who know the facts appreciate the seriousness of the injuries that have been imposed upon the Arab residents of the old British mandate of Palestine. It is easy to find people who can be blamed for the fighting of 1948 and 1967. It is easy to find fault with Israel, with the United States, with King Hussein, with President Nasser, and with other Arab leaders. But Palestinians cannot afford to waste their energies in looking back and in finding fault.

For too many years Palestinians were treated as pawns by world leaders who divided up their country and determined their future without asking for their views or their leave. Worse, for at least the first half of this century the Palestinians treated themselves as pawns. Even after 1948 Palestinians in the refugee camps and elsewhere were waiting for the world to solve the Palestinian problem. Within the last five or six years the situation has changed. Palestinians have decided that they will no longer be content to

wait passively for a future determined by others. They have decided to take their future into their own hands. They have decided
to affect what happens.

It is an exciting and stirring change. The difference between
treating oneself as an object whose role will be determined by
history and treating oneself as a maker of history is more revolu-
tionary than the difference between pursuing one political objective
or another. Within the last half-dozen years this revolution in
thinking has caught hold. What was perhaps the most difficult task
for Palestinian leadership has already been accomplished.

There remains, however, the continuing problem of ends and
means: A national movement needs ends that are far enough in
the future to serve as a guiding star yet near enough at hand to
stir people to practical action. A national movement needs means
that are well adapted to its ends and that make the best use of its
resources. The Palestinian movement has not yet struck a successful balance of ends and means, nor has it made good use of its
resources.

Palestinians are today pursuing a goal that appears wholly unrealistic, by means that appear counterproductive. The goal is to
replace Israel with a Palestinian state. It is proposed to accomplish this exclusively by military means—essentially a war of
attrition through guerrilla and commando acts of physical destruction. To outsiders, and even to many Palestinians, this program has
a fairyland quality of unreality. Despite the real bravery and the
real blood of the Palestinian men and women involved, there is
no appreciable chance of Palestinians destroying the Israeli military forces, which are equally brave. Nor is there a chance that the
Israeli cabinet will meet one morning and vote to dissolve the
state of Israel because of the continuing acts of Palestinian terror.
Even before the Jordanian army was turned on the Palestinian
commandos, Palestinians through military action alone could not
replace Israel with a Palestinian state; today such action offers even
less chance of success, in one year or in a hundred. And, unfortunately, Palestinians have essentially been limiting themselves to
military action.

Palestinians have tied their political arm behind their back.

They have, in effect, taken the position that they are not interested in talking, not interested in negotiations, not interested in a political solution. And yet Palestinians have better political than military weapons. They have legitimate grievances, good friends, and intelligent, articulate, and persuasive spokesmen.

Many Palestinians have made the mistake of believing that they must choose between military and political means. Quite the contrary. Although Palestinians do not have enough military capability to be effective alone, what they do have may well be enough to produce results if combined with political action. While Israel will not be conquered by Palestinian attacks nor will it surrender to them, Israel might well agree to do something in order to be relieved of them. But unless there is some forum in which discussion between Palestinians and others is taking place, a terrorist attack on an Israeli jeep is no more effective than an auto accident. And currently auto accidents kill far more Israelis than do Palestinian terrorists. If Palestinians begin to talk, then—and only then—might Israelis be interested in saying something to them in order to avoid future guerrilla attacks.

A decision to use political capability does not require a decision to abandon all threats of force. Israel did not disband its army upon entering the Jarring talks.

Rather than concentrate on things that Palestinians want to have happen in the future and what they can do to cause them to happen, Palestinians have concentrated on the goal of "unity." It is important to have an organization and to have a political committee that can make decisions. There are, however, major differences within the Palestinian movement, as there are within the Democratic party in the United States or within the Labour party in Britain. In such cases unity is best pursued not as an end in itself. When the issue is unity, colleagues look at each other and note those matters on which they differ. When the issue is an action program, they can set to work on those matters on which they agree.

Instead of "unity," Palestinians should be discussing the means by which they are going to pursue their goal and should be deciding upon some intermediate objectives. They should discuss these in terms of specifics—specific steps Palestinians would like others to take in the foreseeable future, and specific things that Palestinians can do to make those steps more likely. This approach suggests the following action:

1. Step up political participation; the Palestinian voice should be heard in all places where decisions are being made.
2. Restrict military action; physical acts should be used primarily for their political impact.
3. Adopt intermediate political goals; military pain is effective only when an adversary is confronted with realistic political alternatives that are more attractive.

Political Participation

The objective of the Palestine Liberation Organization is to have an impact on the future. Palestinians can affect the future, but they will not be the only ones who do so. Important decisions that affect both the immediate and the long-term future are being made in New York, in Washington, in Jerusalem, in Cairo, and in Amman, to name a few places. To date, the Palestinian voice is barely heard when such decisions are made. Palestinians rightly complain that the Security Council resolution of November 22, 1967, omits all political aspects of the Palestinian problem and talks simply of a "just settlement of the refugee problem." But why is that so? The Palestinian cause was injured by that resolution because the cause was not adequately represented at the United Nations, and in part that is the fault of Palestinians.

Palestinian voices will be best heard if amplified by formal channels. The political arm of the Palestinian struggle will be effective only within political institutions. Formal mechanisms have substantial advantages in terms of visibility, legitimacy, actual impact, and the seriousness with which others must confront the views presented.

Palestinians have stayed away from meetings and talks for fear that their presence would prejudice their position. In fact it is their absence that has seriously prejudiced the Palestinian position. The fear that talking with someone will cause substantial prejudice to the final outcome is routinely exaggerated. In this case in particular, Palestinians will not confer any additional status on Israel by talking to its officials. So far as status is concerned, Palestinians have far more to gain than to lose. So far as substance is concerned, political participation need not commit Palestinians to do anything. It need not commit them to a separate Palestinian state, or to any particular future with Jordan, or to the acceptance of Resolution 242. Nor need it prejudice claims to the whole of Palestine or aspirations to the ultimate goal of achieving a secular democratic state.

In considering how to make the maximum impact at those points where decisions are likely to be made, you will want to think in terms of specific measures the executive committee of the Palestine Liberation Organization could take to increase the Palestinian voice. The following drafts illustrate the kind of options that ought to be considered. Some of these are obviously alternatives to others, but several might be put into effect concurrently.

1. Establish a Political Representative in New York

The executive committee of the Palestine Liberation Organization might send to New York—and perhaps to other places—a prominent and officially authorized representative to speak directly for the executive committee, to convey its views and thinking, to receive proposals, messages, and the views of governments, and to pass them on to the committee. He could also alert the committee to new developments on which it might be desirable for the committee to take a position.

Without such a representative, the Palestinian people are deprived of a significant opportunity for their views to make an impact on matters as they develop. An "information program" to publicize the justness of the Palestinian cause, however desirable, is no substitute. It is one-way; it is not concerned with current action questions; and it does not command much political attention.

Furthermore, without easily available channels for others to reach the executive committee with proposals or to request or receive its views, there is little incentive for most governments to take Palestinian views into account.

At the United Nations today, Palestinians are included in the delegations of some of the Arab states. This does bring Palestinians to the United Nations and gives them certain rights, among them that of speaking in a world forum. An official Palestinian representative might similarly be attached to the delegation of an Arab state, but he would be *the* Palestinian representative, not just a Palestinian. His personal standing and intellectual status within the political structure of the Palestinian movement would be crucial to his success in this role. The more weighty a figure he was within the Palestinian movement the more other governments would be interested in talking with him and in listening to him.

In action terms, such a decision might be reflected in an announcement along the following lines:

DRAFT 1

Announcement of a Palestinian Political Representative in New York

The executive committee of the Palestinian Liberation Organization today released the text of the following letter conveyed by its representative to the Secretary-General of the United Nations:

Dear Mr. Secretary-General:

Present discussions based on Security Council Resolution 242 of November 22, 1967, recognize neither the political rights nor even the existence of the Palestinian people. It is imperative that the world not again attempt to impose on the Palestinian people, those most directly concerned, a "solution" to the problem of Palestine without even considering their views.

Accordingly, the executive committee of the Palestine Liberation Organization, as representative of the legitimate rights and aspirations of the Palestinian people, is sending its official representative, Mr. _____, to be present at the United Nations in order that Palestinian voices may better be heard.

We would like to request that you personally do what you can to bring about such formal or informal improvements in the present format of discussions on the Palestinian question as may be necessary to enable our representative to assist in the full consideration of the rights and views of the Palestinian people.

Sincerely yours,

(Palestine Liberation Organization)

2. Secure Palestinian Representation in the Jordanian Delegation

Another way of having a Palestinian spokesman at the United Nations would be to have Jordan adopt a dual representation approach. King Hussein has said that he must currently look after the interests of the Palestinians of the West Bank, pending their ultimate decision on whether to remain with Jordan.[19] It would be consistent for him to accept responsibility now for seeing that a Palestinian voice is heard at the United Nations. Furthermore, the King might prefer that an official representative of the Palestinian movement sent to New York be under Jordanian auspices rather than those of the Palestinian movement alone or under the auspices of any other state.

After the military action that the Jordanian army has taken against the Palestinian commandos many Palestinians would find it difficult to appear at the United Nations under Jordanian auspices. But it would be an interim situation and deserves consideration. The executive committee of the Palestine Liberation Organization might suggest that Egypt explore with the Jordanian government the possibility of Jordan's adopting this idea and communicating with the Secretary-General in the following vein:

DRAFT 2

Jordanian Letter Suggesting a Palestinian Ambassador at the United Nations as the Jordanian Deputy Representative

Dear Mr. Secretary-General:

As you are well aware, one of the major causes of the current crisis in the Middle East lies in the fact that for generations decisions about what should happen to Palestine have been made without even the participation of representatives of the Palestinian people. Today, again, decisions about the future of the Middle East are being considered, and today, again, there is involved in these consultations no spokesman for the Palestinian people. This cannot be allowed to continue.

The government of Jordan has special responsibilities for the Palestinian people. In international discussions this government must represent the interests of the state of Jordan and, to the best of its ability, the interests of the Palestinian people. To facilitate the carrying out of this dual responsibility, the government of Jordan has made the following decision:

The delegation of Jordan to the United Nations and to any international discussion concerning the Middle East will henceforth be divided between persons who speak for and represent the government of Jordan as such and those who speak for and represent the Palestinian people.

The Permanent Representative of Jordan has been asked to continue to devote his diplomatic and representational efforts to conveying to the United Nations the views of the government of Jordan which do, of course, take into consideration Palestinian views. Beyond this, the government of Jordan has decided to designate as "Deputy Permanent Representative of Jordan to the United Nations and Provisional Spokesman for the Views of the

Palestinian People" an individual selected for this post by the executive committee of the Palestine Liberation Organization. This individual will have full diplomatic status and serve as deputy head of the Jordanian delegation. He will be asked to devote his diplomatic and representational efforts to conveying to the United Nations and to others the views of the Palestinians. He will consult regularly with the full range of Palestinian opinion. In the absence of such authority as the Palestinians may give him, he will not enter into any commitments on their behalf, but he will provide an immediate avenue of communication pending the establishment of better means.

Since no claims of new diplomatic status, double voting rights, or other comparable rights are being advanced, there is no necessity of any decision at this stage by the United Nations or by any of its members. On matters put to a vote the vote will be cast on behalf of the government of Jordan. It is hoped that presiding officers will appreciate the desirability of the action taken by Jordan in making it possible for members better to understand some of the views of those most immediately con-cerned with the future of the Middle East and that during debate they will facilitate this process by recognizing different individuals at different times as "the Representative of Jordan." This practice falls within the well-established precedents where in committee meetings and elsewhere different spoksmen who are experts on different matters speak at different times for the same member.

To further the purposes of the action taken today by the government of Jordan I would like to ask that you circulate a copy of this letter to each member of the United Nations.

Sincerely yours,

_____

Permanent Representative of Jordan

3. Secure a United Nations Representative
to the Palestinians

Because of the present territorial distribution of the Palestinian people and the variety of their views, it is difficult today for any one man to be *the* spokesman for the Palestinian people. One idea that several Palestinians in discussions with me thought might be promising was for the United Nations to designate someone to travel among the Palestinians and to solicit their views. Instead of trying to establish a kind of ambassador *from* the Palestinians, the idea would be to establish a kind of ambassador *to* the Palestinians.

We discussed the thought that the Security Council might ask the Secretary-General to establish an *ad hoc* committee of three, chosen by him after consultations with Palestinians, to formulate and report their views and proposals. Below is an alternative formulation of the same general idea, but asking an individual rather than a committee to perform this function. In either case this idea has some appeal for Palestinians because they are less exposed and there is less danger of their appearing to be committed to something they do not accept. On the other hand, Palestinians would again be treated more as objects than as the active masters of their own fate. The success of the idea would depend upon the energy and talents of the person or persons selected.

The best way to get the United Nations to appoint someone in charge of presenting the Palestinian views and proposals is probably through a Security Council resolution, which could be sponsored by any member of the council. A Palestinian spokesman might see if he could generate interest in a draft along the following lines:

DRAFT 3
Security Council Resolution Establishing a Temporary United Nations Representative to the Palestinians

The Security Council,

Convinced that at the heart of any viable solution to the problems in the Middle East lies the satisfaction of the essential personal and national rights of the Palestinian Arab people and the reconciliation of those rights with the rights of other peoples in the area,

Noting the declarations of the government of Jordan and the concurrence expressed by other governments that the Palestinian people shall have the full right of self-determination,

Recognizing that the Palestinian situation is not a matter essentially within the jurisdiction of any one state,

Concerned that no adequate avenues presently exist for the peaceful participation of Arab Palestinians in the international consideration of their future, the future of Gaza and the West Bank, and in the entire settlement of the Middle East question,

1. *Expresses* the concern and regret of the United Nations for the painful and unjust treatment of so many Palestinians in the past;

2. *Reaffirms* the right of the Palestinian Arab people to a homeland in Palestine as expressed in previous United Nations declarations;

3. *Recognizes* that the boundaries of such a Palestinian homeland, like the boundaries of Israel and other states in the area, and its relationship with Israel, with Jordan, and with other states remain to be worked out on a free and mutually acceptable basis;

4. *Requests* the Secretary-General after consultation with member states in the area to designate a "Special Representative of the United Nations to the Palestinian People" who shall

(a) Consult with the executive committee of the Palestine Liberation Organization and with other groups and individuals reflecting a full diversity of Palestinian views,

(b) Develop proposals for Arab Palestinian participation in international consideration of questions affecting the Palestinians,

(c) Develop proposals for peaceful steps toward achieving realization of the Palestinians' inalienable rights and toward reconciling these rights with the rights of other peoples in the area, and

(d) Report to the Secretary-General from time to time.

4. Engage in Direct Talks with Israel

At some time Palestinians will want to consider the possibility of direct bilateral talks between Israel and the executive committee of the Palestinian Liberation Organization (or perhaps some other Palestinian organization). Such talks might (1) increase the status of the Palestinian organization, (2) demonstrate that Palestinians are not bound by the terms of reference of Resolution 242, and (3) demonstrate that Israel must seek a solution satisfactory to Palestinians as well as to Egypt and Jordan.

If such talks are ever to take place, it is probably better for Palestinians that the talks take place at their initiative than at Israel's. That fact in itself would strengthen the Palestinian hand.

If, after Palestinian positions and proposals had been prepared, such talks seemed desirable, a press release and telegram along the following lines might be issued:

DRAFT 4
Palestinian Invitation to Israel for Direct Discussions

The executive committee of the Palestine Liberation Organization today released the text of the following telegram sent
yesterday to the Foreign Minister of Israel:

> In the United Nations discussions in New York which involve
> Egypt and Jordan, Israel is not dealing with representatives
> of those most directly concerned in the Middle East conflict,
> namely, the Palestinian people. We call upon Israel to meet
> with the executive committee of the Palestine Liberation
> Organization for direct discussions. Purpose of talks is to
> consider all questions of how Christians, Moslems, and Jews
> can best live in peace in Palestine. Basis is that neither side
> need accept in advance the views of the other on any point
> including status. Suggest first meeting be in New York
> beginning at 10:00 A.M. Monday, ——————. Please
> reply to ——————.

An alternative way of inviting Israel to direct talks would be
to suggest a particular topic. An example of this is given below in
the discussion of possible intermediate objectives.

5. Work Toward a Coalition Government in Jordan

The best way, though perhaps the most difficult, for Palestinian
views to be represented in the political processes that will affect
the future is to have those views fully and fairly represented within
the government of Jordan. If the King and the Jordanian army
would be prepared to accept a true coalition government of
Bedouins and Palestinians—a government of reconciliation—
there would be a number of reasons why the idea should be seriously considered by the Palestinians:

• It would reduce the risk of Jordan's undercutting the legitimate interests of the Palestinians.

- It would provide a firm foundation for Palestinian voices to be heard in all international deliberations.
- It would carry forward the generally accepted idea that the West Bank should be under Jordanian sovereignty, at least until freed of Israeli military occupation and until the Palestinian people have chosen otherwise.
- It would provide an increasing number of Palestinian leaders with governmental experience.
- It would provide a transitional period between the absolute monarchy of the past and the socialist or democratic government of the future.

For any such joint or coalition government to work, however, King Hussein would apparently have to alter radically his way of conducting affairs. Ministers in the cabinet would have to be treated as ministers in a constitutional government, with substantial authority, and not merely as "king's men" to be shuffled around or bypassed at the monarch's discretion. The King would also have to convince the army that those whom they have been fighting should now be invited into the government.

For the time being, at least, this idea may seem unrealistic. It might well be kept in mind, however, for under future circumstances a coalition Jordanian government in which Palestinians exercised substantial political power might become a real possibility.

One way to give further consideration to this idea either now or later would be to try to put it into operational form. For example, you might try to draft two statements, one by King Hussein announcing the formation of a "government of reconciliation" and the other by a leading Palestinian political figure explaining why he and his Palestinian colleagues had accepted their ministerial posts in the Jordanian government.

6. Establish a Provisional Government of Palestine

Palestinians have often considered the possibility of establishing a provisional government. Forming such a government would take advantage of the recognition and formal status it might receive from other governments. Forming such a government might also tend to bring the Palestinian question into a somewhat more manageable structure. The Palestinian people, whether in refugee camps, in Gaza, on the West Bank, or elsewhere, are not likely to achieve the best possible result unless there is some generally recognized organizational entity looking after their interests. Many members of the United Nations might recognize a government of Palestine. Many would see in it the best available voice of the Palestinians and the most promising way of converting the present situation into one with which other governments would effectively deal.

Although such a provisional government would presumably be claiming all the territory of the old mandate of Palestine, which includes all of Israel, there would be one unusual feature. It would be claiming territory (and over a quarter of a million people now living on it) that is not claimed to be part of the sovereign territory of any other nation in the world, namely, Gaza. It might be comparatively easy for some states to recognize the provisional government on the ground that whatever its boundaries it is at least the best claimant to Gaza and perhaps also to the West Bank. Once recognized, a provisional government could claim for itself whatever boundaries it wished to claim.

The following is an illustrative draft of a proclamation of such a provisional government:

DRAFT 5
Proclamation of a Provisional Government of Palestine

PROCLAMATION

WHEREAS for generations the Arab people of Palestine have not been permitted by the governments of the world to determine their own fate;

WHEREAS in consequence of the grave injustice inflicted upon the Jewish people by Hitler, colonialist governments that were unwilling to accept Jewish refugees themselves injected hundreds of thousands of Jews into Palestine and established a Zionist state against the will of the Palestinian people who lived there and whose homeland it is;

WHEREAS a grave injustice has been imposed upon the Arab people of Palestine who have been driven from their homes, have been mistreated in refugee camps for decades, and have not been allowed to return to their homes;

WHEREAS once again governments of the world, without any legitimate participation of the Palestinian people, are proposing to reach and impose upon us some alleged solution that does not respect our inalienable rights;

WHEREAS there are portions of Palestine now claimed both by the Palestinian people and by the government of Israel, which has imposed itself upon Palestine but has never obtained the acceptance of the Palestinian people to whom the land truly belongs;

WHEREAS the Palestinian people have organized themselves into a national council that is as representative as possible under present circumstances;

WHEREAS further delay in establishing the true government of Palestine increases the risk of further injustice and further imposition of measures that ignore the rights of the Palestinian people;

WHEREAS only through a provisional government can the Palestinian people ensure that Palestinians now subject to alien rule and hostile military occupation can participate in decisions under which their fate is to be decided;

NOW THEREFORE IT IS HEREBY PROCLAIMED:

1. That the provisional government of Palestine exists effective from 00:00 hours, _____, 197__, Jerusalem time;

2. That this government has all the rights as the sole legitimate successor to the sovereignty of the government of the United Kingdom, upon the termination of the Palestine mandate;

3. That this government is the sole legitimate representative of the Palestinian people in the exercise of their inalienable right of self-determination;

4. That this government is the legitimate custodian of all political rights that have been recognized as belonging to the Palestinian people by resolutions of the United Nations General Assembly;

5. That until this government through formal and uncoerced action should agree, the territory over which this government claims legitimate sovereignty is the entire territory of Palestine; but that this government pledges to work out with the government of Jordan, with whom Palestinians and this government must unite to ensure realization of the rights of all Palestinians, a mutually agreeable tentative relationship between that government and this one, and peaceful and mutually acceptable procedures for determining both the will of the Palestinian people and the ultimate relationship between the government of Jordan and the provisional government of Palestine;

6. That this government now seeks recognition from any friendly government in the world as the legitimate representative of the Palestinian people, without prejudice to questions of secure and recognized boundaries of Palestine or of the eventual juridical relationship between this government and the government of Jordan;

7. That the policy of this government shall be one of justice for all Palestinians and for all other peoples in the area;

8. That this government proposes to seek justice through peaceful means but reserves the right, as do other governments, to use force in self-defense and as permitted under the charter of the United Nations;

9. That this government pledges itself to hold full democratic elections among all Palestinians at the earliest opportunity.
       APPROVED BY THE PALESTINE COUNCIL, and
                signed in witness thereof by

                                    _____

                                    _____

                                    _____

                                    _____

In addition to revisions in Palestinian strategy to permit greater political participation, changes should also be considered in Palestinian military activities.

Military Action

You should carefully think through the consequences of Palestinian terrorist and guerrilla activity to date. Without recommending that any such activities be pursued in the future, let me suggest some of the problems and the kind of analysis that, in my judgment, would have to underlie any rational program of continued guerrilla activity.

Sometimes the purpose of military action is physically to impose a given result. Allied military action against Hitler was directed toward the physical conquest of Germany so that the Allies would have on-the-ground control of the situation. Israeli military force was used in the Sinai and the West Bank with the same kind of purpose: physically to impose a given result within a given geographical area. The military force of the Vietcong applied against South Vietnam and the military force of the United States applied against North Vietnam had a totally different kind of purpose. The Vietcong were not trying to conquer South Vietnam acre by acre. The United States was not seeking to end up in physical control of North Vietnam. Each party was using military force in an effort to exert influence. Each was inflicting pain with the hope of thereby influencing government officials and others to change their minds and to act differently. The Palestinians should recognize that any military force applied by them has this second kind of purpose. The Palestinians have no hope of physically imposing their will on Israel by applying superior military force, acre by acre, until the territory has been conquered. The only purpose for which they could be applying military force is to exert influence. For the Palestinians, military force is rational if and only if the impact it has on people's minds is favorable to the Palestinians.

You should try to estimate the effect of Palestinian guerrilla activity to date on the three audiences of concern to you: Israelis, third parties, and the Palestinian people themselves. My estimate would be that on the first two audiences the effect has been wholly counterproductive; on the Palestinians the effect has been mixed.

Commando and guerrilla activities have been directed against targets of opportunity, including a supermarket and a bus, but are by and large focused on military personnel and equipment. The Israeli public seems to interpret such actions as conveying this message:

This is a war between Palestinians and Israel. Unless Israel disbands itself and turns the country over to a nonexistent Palestinian government, we Palestinians will continue to kill a few innocent Israelis as long as we can.

The message is wholly unpersuasive. In a war between Palestinians and Israel all Israelis know which side they are on. Wars are settled by military force, and Israelis also know which side has superior military force. The demand that Israel disappear strikes Israelis as wholly unreasonable. The occasional killing and wounding of Israelis in pursuit of this program appears outrageous. The Palestinian military operations do not impose enough costs on Israel to affect its military capability but do impose enough to cause all Israelis, including many who are generally critical of their government, to side with the government against the Palestinians. Random mortar shells from Lebanon, random rockets into an Israeli town, and random ambushes within Israel or Gaza tend to convince people that in order to have a civilized life the efforts of the Israeli army to destroy the Palestinian guerrillas must be supported.

The effect on the United States and other third parties is similar. Any sympathy for the Palestinian cause tends to be outweighed by sympathy for Israeli citizens faced with irrational terror.

I would guess that the results on Palestinians themselves are mixed. There is an uplifting effect from seeing brave men take daring action. At last Palestinians are doing something! Commandos and guerrillas become the heroes of all Palestinians. Yet the very futility of the military action must be discouraging. Not many Palestinians criticize it, but many see the military road as hopeless. Among Palestinians a small number of dedicated men become increasingly committed through action to a continuation of the military struggle. A larger group of Palestinians remain comparatively passive. There is a risk that, like the anarchists of Spain who continue after more than a generation to fight the Franco regime, these dedicated men will continue to perform their destructive acts, despite the fact that such activities become unrelated to the future and to the broad political cause from which they arose.

In considering what kinds of military action if any might help the Palestinian cause, a political purpose should be defined, and the action tailored to suit that purpose. One possible approach, for example, might be along the following lines.

You might pick as intermediate objectives (1) convincing large numbers of Israeli citizens of the justice of the Palestinian cause and (2) reducing the extent to which the Arab cause is prejudiced by Israel's program of "changing the facts" through new Israeli construction in Arab communities. Those are not in any sense ultimate objectives from the Palestinian point of view, but attaining them would be more important to the realization of ultimate Palestinian objectives than would attaining some purely military intermediate objective such as one hundred dead Israeli soldiers or ten fewer Israeli jeeps.

To convince Israeli citizens of the justice of the Palestinian cause it will help to call attention to specific Israeli actions that are now going on and that ought to be stopped. The impact upon Israelis will be more constructive if Palestinians can avoid doing things that appear to be unjustified or excessive. Do not try to bite off too much at once. Concentrate on one issue, and if successful there, go on to another. Vietnamese opponents of the United States concentrated their political attack first on the aerial bombing of North Vietnam, and gained major political support for stopping the bombing. After the bombing had been stopped they concentrated their efforts on withdrawal of United States forces, again gaining political support for this action from large numbers of Americans.

A good political target for Palestinian action would appear to be the Israeli program for constructing new permanent buildings for Israelis in Arab territory occupied through military force in June 1967. A Palestinian program might involve the following elements:

Articulate the demand. "Stop the construction," like "Stop the bombing," could become a clearly focused and oft-repeated demand. It could become a cause. It could become a continuing issue within Israel, dividing some Israelis from others.

Legitimate the demand. An information program could make it eminently clear that the demand for stopping Israeli construction in Arab territory is a reasonable and legitimate request. United Nations resolutions already tend to support this position, and more could be adopted. Much international law here is also on the side of the Palestinians. Governments of third states and writers could be encouraged to gather and to publish facts about the apparently illegal Israeli conduct.

Communicate the warning. The Israeli *public* could get the impression that further Israeli construction in occupied territory, instead of helping Israel, would create a risk of aggravating a bad situation and of intensifying Arab hostility. The Israeli *government* could get the impression that it would lose popular support if it continued the construction program.

Make the warning credible. Physical acts by Palestinians should be intended to convince the Israeli public and third parties of the legitimacy of the Palestinian cause and the seriousness of the risks for Israel if it ignores reasonable Palestinian demands. As suggested above, military activities to date by Palestinians have, in my judgment, been harmful to the Palestinian cause. What sticks in people's minds is that Palestinians blow up school buses and kill civilians. In an attempt to convince people of the seriousness of the Palestinian cause you have convinced them of the illegitimacy of your methods. The guerrilla program should be carefully reviewed.

The first and most important task is to stop activities that kill and injure. The American radicals who blew up a University of Wisconsin research facility killed a graduate student in the process. The public reaction against this senseless killing of an innocent man created a substantial backlash against the radical cause. In subsequent bombings radicals made elaborate efforts to avoid such casualties by giving telephone warnings of impending explosions. (Even so, the bombings have had a negative effect on the radical cause, perhaps because the destruction had so little relationship to any legitimate issue.) Acts of wanton terror are no way to advance your cause.

There is a world of difference between such acts and a military program narrowly directed at the rational destruction of carefully selected inanimate objects in order to further a political purpose. A program of sabotage, for example, that was narrowly directed to prevent the further construction by Israel of facilities on the West Bank, hotels in Sharm el Sheikh, or oil wells in the Sinai might conceivably serve two purposes: It could call attention to the grievance, and it could demonstrate the unacceptability of such construction to Palestinians. Furthermore, it would attack Israel at a point where it is politically vulnerable. Both the international community and some Israelis might be expected to support a move to stop Israeli construction in occupied lands. Some workers might even refuse to work on such projects. If there is to be a use of explosives by Palestinians such use might be narrowly directed at Israeli structures in occupied territories intended to facilitate Israeli expansion.

In any such activity you should accept the moral and political responsibility of avoiding any loss of life. There are ways of avoiding the loss of life, as Israel demonstrated in its famous raid on the Beirut airport.[20] (You should be able to do better than Israel did there if you limit any destruction to legitimate targets—objects that in themselves have something morally wrong about them.) The purpose of any military action by you lies in its political impact, which means that planning, timing, great discretion, and skill are crucial. I am not saying that you *should* engage in any act of violence; I am saying that you should *not* engage in the kind of wide-ranging anti-Israeli violence that creates both human suffering and an anti-Palestinian reaction.

Intermediate Goals

As already indicated, intimately related to the problems of increasing political participation and of restricting military action is the problem of adopting and articulating realistic intermediate goals for the Palestinian movement. To adopt intermediate goals is not to abandon ultimate ones. To hope to stop Israeli construction in occupied territory sets no more of an effective limit on Palestinian objectives than the goal of constructing those buildings sets an effective limit on Israeli objectives.

The executive committee should regard as one of its most important tasks the definition of some intermediate goals in a form that suggests who is to do what about them in the immediate future. Two more illustrations of the kind of intermediate goals that Palestinians might adopt are the following:

1. Civil Rights for Palestinians Under Occupation

One of the vulnerable aspects of the Israeli military occupation lies in the denial of some political and civil rights to Arab residents. The Israeli government is sensitive on the subject of denying civil rights to Arabs under its military rule. The maintenance of preventive detention and the reluctance to permit an Arab university on the West Bank are subjects of discussion within Israel. You should, I believe, seek to formulate some specific plan in a form capable of decision by the Israeli government that would grant Arabs under Israeli military rule freedom to engage in real political activity. One way of pursuing this goal would be to publish something along the following lines:

DRAFT 6

Palestinian Appeal for Civil Rights in Occupied Territory

The executive committee of the Palestine Liberation Organization today issued the following appeal to the government of Israel:

Today one million Palestinians remain under the military rule of the government of Israel. On one ground or another the government of Israel has retained its military grip and in violation of the standards of every civilized society has deprived human beings of their basic rights. Whatever the final outcome of the Middle East conflict shall be, about which our views are well known, we demand an immediate improvement in present conditions.

On behalf of all Arabs under Israeli rule, we demand:

1. Freedom of speech and press. No one should fear punishment for what he says or writes.
2. An end to preventive detention. It is outrageous that a government claiming to be a model of democracy should insist upon the power of preventive detention without charges or public trial.
3. Freedom of petition. Individuals should be free to formulate petitions and to circulate them for signature and support. Is Israel afraid even to hear what the people think?
4. Freedom of education. Arabs must be free to establish a university on the West Bank.

5. Freedom to travel. Palestinians must be free to visit other countries and to return to the West Bank without special permits. An "exit only" policy cannot be justified on any ground.
6. Freedom of assembly. Even today Israel prevents Arab mayors and other civilians from holding open public meetings to discuss problems of common interest.
7. A political free zone on the West Bank. As much as possible of the West Bank should be designated as a political zone free from Israeli rule, within which Palestinians can carry on self-government and engage in the political organizational activities that are essential to coherent Palestinian decisions about the future of the Palestinian people.

We call on Israel to grant these basic rights immediately, and without reservation.

We call on those Israeli citizens who believe in minimal civil and human rights to insist that their government meet these demands.

We call on friends of Israel throughout the world to see that their funds and their assistance are not used to support preventive detention and the denial of civil rights to Palestinians under Israeli military rule.

2. A Common State as an Intermediate Goal

One of the most intriguing ideas that may affect the future of the Arab-Israeli conflict is one advanced by Professor Gidon Gottlieb.[21] His idea is that there might at some point in the not too distant future be a common state of Palestine that would include within it two substates, one Arab and one Jewish, each having its own measure of sovereignty. There are an endless number of possible variations on the idea. One is illustrated by the following

draft, which spells out some substantive ideas as an agenda for
proposed direct talks with Israel:

DRAFT 7
Palestinian Proposal for a Common State of Palestine
Consisting of Arab and Jewish Substates

The Honorable
The Minister of Foreign Affairs
Government of Israel
Jerusalem
Dear Mr. Minister:

On behalf of the executive committee of the Palestine
Liberation Organization, I would like to invite you to participate
in an exploratory discussion with us about a possible future
for Palestine, one to be achieved by peaceful means and one
that would fully assure the legitimate interests of Israel as well
as those of the Palestinian people.

The purpose of the discussion is to see if it might be possible
to identify an intermediate goal, perhaps two years away, which
looks sufficiently promising for us to undertake the actual
negotiations and the drafting of documents necessary to bring
it about. The idea we would like to discuss is that of a sovereign
common state consisting of two substates, also sovereign, one
Arab and one Jewish. As a background for our preliminary
discussion we have enumerated the following points, which
might serve as a basis for discussion.

1. The whole of Palestine as it existed under the British
mandate in 1947 shall be one country, the national home of two
peoples.
2. Jordan might or might not become part of this common state.

3. The juridically sovereign Common State of Palestine would be composed of two component states, each sovereign and equal, based on the exercise by the Palestinian Arab people and by the Jewish people of their respective rights of self-determination.

4. The Jewish component state (Israel) and the Arab component state would each be a member of the United Nations. (It is possible that the Common State of Palestine would also become a United Nations member, just as the Soviet Union is a member while two of its "sovereign" component states, the Ukraine and Byelorussia, are members.)

5. The governments of the two component states would agree upon boundaries, economic affairs, and mutually satisfactory security arrangements. Our position would be that the boundaries should be as defined in the United Nations partition of 1948, but that this issue, like other matters, would be subject to negotiation.

6. The governments of the two component states would agree upon the structure, powers, jurisdiction, and authority of the government of the Common State of Palestine. Initially the Common State would have no territory under its direct authority except for a "capital district" located in Jerusalem. Initially the Common State would have the power to act only with the concurrence of both of the two component states. It would have additional limited powers to coordinate activities of the two component states, to recommend action to them, and to prepare recommendations for the transfer of additional authority over time from the component states to the Common State.

7. Citizens of the two component states would at the same time be citizens of the Common State. Return of Arabs and Jews to their component states would be governed by the domestic law

of each state, as designed to protect its national and ethnic character.

8. It would be contemplated that over succeeding years collaboration between the two component states would become closer and the powers of the Common State would increase, but that would be up to subsequent decision of the two component states.

We believe that these enumerated points adequately suggest the general proposal we would like to discuss with you.

As you well know, our goal for Palestine is a democratic secular state in which Christians, Moslems, and Jews can live as equals with none having a special status. As you must also know, we are prepared to work for generations, if need be, to achieve that goal, and we are prepared to use force, if need be, to move toward it.

Our thought is that if agreement could now be reached on the Common State of Palestine, the Arab component state would then commit itself to using only peaceful political means to pursue the gradual merger of the two substates.

To explore these ideas further we invite you personally or, if you are unable to attend, someone designated by you to meet with us beginning at 10:30 A.M. on Tuesday the _____ of _____ at the Cyprus Hilton Hotel in Nicosia.

Sincerely yours,

_____

(Palestine Liberation Organization)

Well, if you agree with nothing in this letter it may still have served its purpose by stimulating you to think more clearly about what it is that you would like to have happen during the next six months or two years, and what you can do to make its happening more likely.

With the thought that this letter contains ideas of possible interest to a wider audience, I am planning to publish it (with names omitted) together with comparable letters that I have written to others involved in the Middle East problem. If you have reactions, comments, or criticisms I would welcome them. Needless to say there is no implication that any one agrees with anything I have written.

Sincerely yours,

ROGER FISHER

5.
Letter to a Jordanian

August 23, 1971

Dear _____ [an official of the government of Jordan],

I have been going through the exercise of applying theories that I set forth in "Fractionating Conflict" and *International Conflict for Beginners* to each of several major protagonists in the Arab-Israeli conflict and have been writing out the kind of advice that might stimulate them to think through what they ought to be doing.

Jordan has three main targets of influence: the Palestinians, Israel, and third parties. In each case the government, and particularly the King, should identify some short-term objective—one that might be accomplished within, say, six months to a year—and see what can be done toward achieving it.

Keeping the Palestinians In

Jordan's general objectives are to have Israeli troops withdraw from territories occupied in 1967, to have the West Bank and East Jerusalem restored to Jordan (and perhaps to acquire Gaza as well), and to have the Palestinians freely and overwhelmingly decide that they and their territory should be within the Hashemite Kingdom of Jordan. Jordan would like these events to take place as rapidly as possible. The passage of time may not only weaken the King's position, it is likely to weaken the ties that the West Bank has with Jordan.

In regard to this objective, it is to Jordan's interest that Palestinian leaders see their future and the future of the Palestinian people as closely tied with that of Jordan. Even though the Jordanian army subdued the Palestinian commandos in September 1970 and again in July 1971, there is apparently no universal conviction among the Palestinians that the break is final. Many still look for the future unity of the East and West banks of the Jordan River. But Jordan had better act to keep the Palestinians involved with Jordan and to keep as many of them as possible looking forward to a future within Jordan's boundaries.

If in early 1970 the King had asked the Palestinians to share in the responsibilities of government, it would have looked as though he were yielding to military power. Commandos were freely roaming the streets of Amman, armed with machine guns, and receiving popular support. The military action of the Jordanian army apparently eliminated the Palestinian commandos within Jordan as a military force. Today if the King asks Palestinians to share in the responsibilities of government he will be doing so from strength, not from weakness.

Bringing effective Palestinian leadership into the government of Jordan would apparently require three major items of persuasion:

- Persuading Palestinian leaders to accept government positions,
- Persuading the Jordanian army to accept the coalition, and
- Persuading the King to let cabinet ministers have some real political power

These are difficult matters, and the question of timing may be crucial. But if Jordan looks forward to a future in which West Bank and other Palestinians decide to cast their lot permanently with Jordan, then someday the monarchy will have to become less autocratic and more constitutional, and the Palestinian population will have to have a substantial say within the government. The sooner that day comes, the more likely Palestinians are to cast their lot permanently with Jordan.

One way to move in this direction would be for Jordan to initiate some discussions with the executive committee of the Palestine Liberation Organization or with a group of individual Palestinian leaders. The temptation on both sides will be to discuss immediate military matters respecting the commandos and the Jordanian army. Of greater importance would be political discussions that might be defined in a public announcement along the following lines:

DRAFT 1

Jordanian Invitation to Palestinians for Political Discussions

The government of Jordan today announced that a group of Palestinian political leaders would be coming to Amman later this month for political discussions about the continuing relationship between Jordan and the Palestinian movement.

The purpose of the discussions is to consider means for closer collaboration during the months ahead in order to hasten the day when the Palestinian people are restored to the possession of their full rights.

It is recognized that there have in the past been some differences of opinion between the government of Jordan and leaders of the Palestinian movement, and that some differences of opinion are bound to occur in the future. Nevertheless, the people of Palestine and the people of the Hashemite Kingdom are in many ways one and the same; they have had a long past in close association and will certainly be in close association for a long future. Furthermore, although the simple withdrawal of Israeli troops from territory occupied in 1967 will in no way constitute an adequate solution to the problem of justice for the Palestinian people, there is widespread agreement that such withdrawal is necessary and should take place as soon as possible.

In these circumstances it is desirable that the leaders of the

Palestinian movement and the leaders of Jordan work in close cooperation. Among the possibilities to be explored are the establishment in Amman of a political headquarters for the Palestine National Council and the reconstitution of the cabinet of the government of Jordan so as to assure that the government fully reflects Palestinian views.

The discussions are expected to proceed for several days, to recess for a period of consultation, and to resume for several days on a later occasion. No announcements are expected until the discussions have concluded.

An Interim Agreement with Israel for the West Bank

To exert influence on Israel, Jordan should act to create occasions for decision and should identify some possible decisions that would move events in the desired direction. While talks have taken place in pursuit of an interim agreement between Egypt and Israel, nothing has been done about an interim agreement between Jordan and Israel. Jordan should urgently consider what kind of an interim agreement it might like, and it should then prepare and discuss a draft. International political pressure from the United States or elsewhere can have little effect on Israel unless there is some specific pending decision that Israel can reasonably be asked to make.

One reasonable interim objective would be to get the bulk of the West Bank back under Jordanian jurisdiction prior to final agreement on the withdrawal of Israeli forces and on such boundary changes in the Latrun and Jerusalem areas as might later be accepted. The following draft suggests one way to go forward toward such an interim agreement:

DRAFT 2

Jordanian Proposal for an Interim Agreement Restoring Most of the West Bank to Its Civil Administration

Secretary-General

United Nations

New York, New York

Dear Mr. Secretary-General:

Under Security Council Resolution 242 of November 22, 1967, your Special Representative is to assist efforts to achieve a peaceful and accepted settlement in accordance with the provisions and principles of that resolution. We would like to ask you to make your Special Representative available for some particular assistance at this time.

We believe that for any final settlement to be durable and acceptable to some of the people most directly concerned, namely, the Arab residents of the West Bank, they must have played a role in the decisions leading up to that final settlement. The residents of the West Bank are currently under Israeli military rule with no political freedom to meet and consider the options available, and no freedom to go back and forth between Amman and their homes. In these circumstances they are unable to consider, let alone accept, a boundary between the West Bank and Israel. They are unable to decide to continue to remain as part of Jordan, as we confidently expect, or to try to work out some other future. If Israel insists upon militarily ruling the West Bank until a final settlement, there is indeed no hope of peace, since Israeli military rule precludes the free choice of any future on the part of a million Arabs.

We therefore conclude that an interim agreement should be reached permitting a resumption of Jordanian civil administration over the bulk of the West Bank in the immediate future, prior to definitive agreement on security and boundary matters. We would like to ask that your Special Representative assist efforts to achieve a peaceful settlement by preparing a draft of an actual interim agreement, a draft he would be ready to recommend to the parties concerned. The interim agreement would include provisions covering the following points:

1. The entire West Bank shall be returned to Jordanian civil administration with the exception of Jerusalem (which shall be the subject of special discussion) and small temporary security zones to be designated by Israel along the Jordan River and along the Israeli frontier in which Israeli military forces may for the time being remain and which shall be under their control and military jurisdiction.

2. During the period of the interim agreement the Jordanian government shall deploy no military units or equipment within the West Bank, but may have police equipped with weapons no larger than side arms or rifles.

3. Israeli military units may remain in control of points for crossing the Jordan River, may inspect all individuals, vehicles, and goods coming into the West Bank, and may confiscate all arms, explosives, and other military equipment from anyone attempting to bring them into the West Bank, but may not bar any unarmed individual from coming in. Israeli military shall notify Jordan of entering persons suspected of terrorist or other illegal activity and may detain them for not over six hours before turning them over to Jordanian authorities. Thereafter the Jordanian government shall be responsible for their disposition.

4. Israeli military units, personnel, and equipment shall have free access on designated roads across the West Bank to and from temporary security zones.

5. The governments of Jordan and Israel shall each designate liaison officers who shall establish a joint office where they can work together to deal with problems that arise; they shall make joint recommendations as to how individual matters shall be dealt with and shall report to their respective governments as necessary.

6. The interim agreement and arrangements pursuant to it are designed to facilitate the implementation of Security Council Resolution 242, especially a just settlement of the refugee problem, and shall be without prejudice to rights or claims of any party with respect to any of the issues involved in the final implementation of that resolution.

We believe that it should be possible to negotiate an interim agreement along these lines without delay. We note that in accepting Secretary Rogers' letter of June 19, 1970, the government of Israel, like the government of Jordan, has committed itself to discussions to be held under the auspices of your Special Representative "according to such procedure and at such places and times" as he may recommend. We urge the prompt preparation of a draft agreement by your Special Representative covering the points specified above, and we request his assistance in negotiating its conclusion.

Sincerely yours,

————————————————

(Government of Jordan)

A Working Party on Jerusalem

Another form of interim agreement would be one establishing procedures for converting Jerusalem from a complicated international muddle (where continued administration by Israel is the easiest and hence the most likely outcome) into a manageable problem through the preparation of a set of proposals for dealing with its different aspects. If Jordan waits for Israel to propose international consideration of Jerusalem, it will never take place. In the meantime the facts will change in Jerusalem to such an extent that achieving a satisfactory and peaceful solution will be more difficult than ever.

A working party on Jerusalem might be set up under a wide variety of auspices. Britain or France might initiate such a project. A private foundation or a religious organization might be persuaded to take the lead. Or perhaps Jordan could encourage Ambassador Jarring to set up a subcommittee on Jerusalem. One way to do this would be to have Jordan give to the Special Representative of the Secretary-General appointed under Resolution 242 a draft of a proposed agreement setting up such a subcommittee:

DRAFT 3

Jordanian-Israeli Interim Agreement Establishing a Subcommittee on Jerusalem

Israel and Jordan agree to the establishment of a subcommittee of the Jarring talks that shall be composed as provided in Part I below and that shall develop a plan for Jerusalem in accordance with the guidelines set forth in Part II and prepare nonbinding working drafts of the operational documents specified in Part III.

Part I

The subcommittee shall be composed of:

—Three persons selected by the government of Israel;

—Three persons selected by the government of Jordan; and

—One person appointed by the Special Representative of the Secretary-General and acceptable to both governments, who shall be the chairman of the subcommittee.

Part II

The parties agree that the draft documents to be prepared by the subcommittee shall reflect the following principles and guidelines:

1. Jerusalem shall be a unified, undivided city composed of two boroughs, one Arab and the other Jewish. The boundaries of the city shall be specified and shall be similar to those of the enlarged municipality now administered by Israel.

2. There shall be no barriers to free movement of any kind within the city or between one borough and the other. Such customs or passport control barriers as either Israel or Jordan may establish shall be placed along the boundary between the city and that state.

3. Each borough shall have its own mayor and borough council elected by the qualified voters resident within that borough.

4. There shall be a Jerusalem City Council or Technical Coordinating Council composed of representatives selected by each borough council and by a Commission on Holy Places. The City Council shall coordinate public services and town planning and shall have such limited authority as may be necessary or desirable to administer the city as a whole, having respect for the desirability of substantial autonomy for each of the boroughs. It shall be contemplated that the Jerusalem City Council may be granted additional authority by Israel and Jordan from time to time in the light of experience.

5. There shall be a Commission on Holy Places, composed of representatives of various religious groups, that shall have defined responsibilities with respect to designated Holy Places.

6. Division of legislative and executive authority among the governments of Israel and Jordan, the Jerusalem City Council,

and the two borough councils shall be worked out and incorporated in a city charter.

7. All divisions of jurisdiction and authority shall be resolved without regard to the question of "sovereignty" but rather with a view to providing the most practical solution to the complex problems involved. After these practical problems have been resolved the nominal boundary between Israel and Jordan may be taken as the line between the two boroughs, but no practical consequence shall follow from this fact; the practical problems will all have been dealt with on their independent merits.

Part III

In accordance with the principles and guidelines set out in Part II above, the subcommittee shall prepare nonbinding drafts of the following documents for consideration by the governments of Israel and Jordan:

1. Jerusalem City Charter
2. Charter of the Arab Borough
3. Charter of the Jewish Borough
4. Legislation respecting Jerusalem to be adopted by Israel
5. Legislation respecting Jerusalem to be adopted by Jordan
6. Treaty between Israel and Jordan respecting Jerusalem
7. Resolution to be adopted by the General Assembly
8. Resolution to be adopted by the Security Council

These thoughts and these drafts will have well served their purpose if they stimulate some political action by the government of Jordan that is designed to affect what happens next, even if that action is quite different from anything I have suggested. Those who act affect what happens; those who do not act let the future be determined by others.

With the thought that this letter contains ideas of possible interest to a wider audience, I am planning to publish it (with your name omitted) together with comparable letters that I have written to others involved in the Middle East problem. I will send you copies of those letters. Needless to say there is no implication that you or anyone else agrees with anything that I have written.

With warm personal regards,

ROGER FISHER

6.
Letter to the United Nations

August 25, 1971

Dear ⸻ [an official of the United Nations],

Since last talking with you I have made, during July, one more trip to the Middle East. I remain convinced that Israel's refusal to agree with Ambassador Jarring's February letter—Israel's position that it will *not* withdraw from all of the Sinai occupied in 1967 —should not be accepted as producing a deadlock. Negotiations would have been easier if Israel had said yes, but Israel has reasons for not committing itself to total withdrawal from the Sinai at the present time when distrust is so high and when no security arrangements have been worked out.

There is much that can be done and should be done about improving the situation in the Middle East, and the United Nations could be taking the lead. Security Council Resolution 242 gives the Secretary-General, through his Special Representative, a continuing mandate "to promote agreement and assist efforts to achieve a peaceful and accepted settlement."

Since returning from the Middle East I have written to people there with whom I spoke, suggesting, in a memorandum and long letters, the approach of working forward piece by piece. Enclosed are copies of this material.

If you have time to look through these letters you will note that two suggestions stand out:

1. Work should be directed less toward the principles of a final settlement and more toward specific, operational steps pro-

ducing tangible results in the weeks ahead—results that will move the Middle East toward a period of peace with justice.

2. Work should proceed concurrently on a number of issues.

If the Secretary-General or his successor should decide to undertake further efforts under Resolution 242, the United Nations should probably make the most of the acceptance by Israel, Egypt, and Jordan of Secretary Rogers' letter of June 19, 1970, proposing discussions under the auspices of the Secretary-General's Special Representative "according to such procedure and at such places and times as [he] may recommend, taking into account as appropriate each side's preference as to method of procedure and previous experience between the parties."

In the light of this agreement the Secretary-General would seem to be free to give new instructions to his Special Representative along the following lines:

DRAFT

Revised Instructions of the Secretary-General to His Special Representative

Dear Mr. Ambassador:

To guide you as you promote agreement and assist efforts to achieve a peaceful and accepted settlement in accordance with the provisions and principles of Security Council Resolution 242 of November 22, 1967, I authorize, and suggest that you may wish to undertake, the following action:

1. Provide representatives of Egypt, Israel, and Jordan with a list of matters for concurrent discussion, such as the following:

WORKING AGENDA

(Discussions shall proceed concurrently on all of the following points.)

I. Preliminary Work
   A. *Palestinian participation.* Possible agreement on procedures to assure participation of Palestinian

representatives in consideration of refugee questions and all other matters as appropriate.

B. *Fund for refugees.* Possible agreement to request the World Bank or some other organization to initiate a fund into which deposits could be placed immediately for the purpose of providing economic and other assistance needed in order to locate Palestinian refugees in permanent homes.

C. *Subcommittee on special matters.* Possible agreement to establish three subcommittees, each instructed to prepare nonbinding draft proposals governing one of the following areas:
   1. Security arrangements in the Sinai to be in effect during and after withdrawal
   2. Jerusalem
   3. Refugees

D. *Interim arrangements with respect to Gaza.* Possible agreement on ways of determining the wishes of the residents of Gaza and dealing with the situation there pending final settlement.

E. *Construction in occupied territory.* Possible agreement on interim limitations on Israeli construction and settlement in occupied territories pending final accord.

II. The Comprehensive Settlement

A. *Documents to be prepared.* Possible agreement on a list of documents to be included in the comprehensive settlement and a brief description of what each document should cover.

B. *Negotiating procedures.* Agreement on the parties to be involved and on the form, manner, and timing of the negotiations for each document.

III. Subsequent Steps and Measures

Possible agreement among the parties on steps that will be necessary to implement and confirm the comprehensive settlement, to assure compliance with its terms, to deal with problems and disputes that may later arise, and to consider improvements in its terms that changed circumstances may make desirable.

2. Inform the parties that any of them may at any time add to the list one or more additional matters for discussion.

3. Inform the parties that you intend to discuss with each party all matters on the list, in any sequence the party may prefer.

4. Make available to the parties for the purpose of their study and thinking drafts, guidelines, or other specific proposals that may be made available to you by members of the Security Council and such other drafts prepared by the Secretariat staff or others as you may think helpful. I am suggesting not that you now prepare or endorse drafts that reflect your personal views, but rather that you arrange to provide the parties with a number of alternative draft approaches for discussion. This will avoid asking any party either to prepare a "position" of its own (from which it might later find it difficult to resile) or to accept the "position" of another party as the basis for negotiation.

5. Establish working subcommittees to deal with different issues, each party being represented by different individuals on the various subcommittees so that they can work concurrently, which should speed the work and make it less likely that any one impasse will bring all negotiations to a halt.

If at any time you feel that additional suggestions or clarification of your authority might be helpful, do not hesitate to ask.

Sincerely yours,

————————————

(Secretary-General)

It seems to me that such guidance and assurance as to his authority might be extremely helpful to the special representative.

In writing to you, as in writing the other letters that are enclosed, I am not seeking secretly to exert influence in one direction or another, or to come up with some special new draft that is going to "solve" the Arab-Israeli conflict. Rather I am trying to suggest a somewhat different approach from that which has been pursued, in the hope that this new approach would provide a more productive way of carrying on the conflict. I recognize that international civil servants, even more than national ones, are closely confined in what they can properly do by the understanding of those around them as to what they ought to be doing. Some of the interested spectators impose serious constraints on those directly involved.

With the thought that these letters contain ideas of possible interest not only to you but also to those "spectators," I am planning to publish them (omitting in each case the name and title of the addressee). My optimistic belief is that the more widely ideas are criticized and discussed, the greater the chance that better ideas will be advanced and pursued.

Sincerely yours,

ROGER FISHER

7.
Letter to an American

September 1, 1971

Dear _____ [an official of the government of the United States],

I continue to admire the energy and persistence with which the United States government is playing the peacemaking role in the Middle East.

You may be interested in the enclosed copies of long letters I have written to Egyptian, Israeli, Palestinian, and other friends concerned with the Arab-Israeli conflict. Although some of the examples are new, the theme is one with which you are familiar:

Be operational. Break up the problem and get to work on the pieces. Figure out what, realistically, you want to have happen during the next few months and then do what you can to make those events more likely.

Most of my thinking as to the approach the United States should take is implicit in suggestions made to others. Let me emphasize two of those points, and then raise a new one.

Concurrent Work on Several Questions

One of the disappointing consequences of the United States government's efforts to obtain an interim agreement permitting the opening of the Suez Canal was that all other work on the

Arab-Israeli conflict apparently came to a stop. Ambassador Jarring went off to Moscow to resume his duties as Swedish Ambassador to the Soviet Union. Everyone else did nothing, waiting to see what the outcome of the United States' efforts would be. As valuable as one interim agreement is, work on it should not be taken as a substitute for work on all other aspects of the problem.

One way to have work proceeding concurrently on a number of different matters is to have different people working on them. There has been some talk of having negotiations proceed "on two or more tracks," and fears have been expressed of getting wires crossed or having too many cooks spoil the broth. But metaphors are no substitute for clear consideration of this problem. There are risks in having different officials within each government—in Washington, in Cairo, and in Jerusalem—working on questions that are related. But the risk of not having them do so seems even greater. To have all issues between Israel and the Arabs meet at a single point of confrontation emphasizes the warlike stance of the parties involved. Among nations at peace there are many different contacts, and many issues are being dealt with concurrently. Dealing with many issues concurrently is a way of making a situation more peaceful.

If the United States is going to fulfill its peacemaking role, perhaps one official should be charged with promoting the opening of the Suez Canal, a different officer given full-time responsibility for promoting the permanent settlement on the West Bank of all Palestinians who would like to live there, a third officer given responsibility for moving forward with respect to Jerusalem, and so forth.

Confronting the Parties with "Yesable Propositions"

There is no chance that the parties will make peace without the help of outsiders. There is also no possibility that any outsider can "impose" a peace upon them. Exerting influence is all we can hope for. As you know, I believe that one of the major ways of exerting influence is to construct a choice, and to confront a party with that choice. To maximize the chance that that choice will be accepted, there should be a political cost in turning it down. If you are confident that Israel, for example, would reject a reasonable proposal, then you might well conclude that there is no point in formally submitting the proposal to that country. What I want to suggest now is that there may well be a point in publicly and formally submitting the proposal even if you are confident that it is going to be turned down.

Some of the major support on which Israel counts is that of its friends in the United States. If confidential diplomatic efforts to open the Suez Canal fail, Israel pays no real price. The failure of negotiations is no one's fault. On the other hand, if after months of negotiations a friendly third party advances the best proposal he can devise, and Israel or Egypt turns it down, that country begins to pay a price. One *no* may not cost it much in terms of its reputation with its friends, but a series of *noes* in response to a series of fair and reasonable proposals might convince a lot of people that that side was not really interested in a fair peace. If American supporters of Israel, for example, began to feel that way, Israel would be under substantial political pressure to say yes to the next reasonable proposal. Comparable benefits from submitting a specific proposal—or a series of specific proposals—even if turned down, should apply to the Arab side as well.

Working with the USSR

The thought that does not appear elsewhere in the enclosed materials is the possibility that the United States might work more closely with the Soviet Union in devising and promoting specific steps toward peace in the Middle East. Granted that Soviet and American interests are not identical; neither are Arab and Israeli interests. If we are trying to get them to cooperate more closely, we ourselves might try to cooperate more closely with the Soviet Union, particularly in the Middle East, where superpower involvement has dangerously complicated an already tragic situation.

One way to reduce the risk of superpower confrontation in the

Middle East is to try to settle the Arab-Israeli conflict. Another way to reduce that risk is to work jointly with the USSR in that task. You will recall how upset the Soviet Union was with the unilateral quality of the United States initiative of June 19, 1970. The cease-fire which that initiative led to was offset in some degree, I fear, by an increased perception both here and in the Soviet Union that in the Middle East the two superpowers were essentially not partners for peace, but rivals.

One way to reduce the perception of hostility would be to discuss in advance with the Soviet Union moves the United States is contemplating. The Soviet Union need not be asked to commit itself or to endorse our moves, but the very process of discussion should further the United States objective of reducing the risk of superpower confrontation in the Middle East.

Another, and less orthodox, way of pursuing the same objective might be to ask the Soviet Union to designate perhaps two staff officers to work with two American staff officers in generating ideas and suggestions as to what ought to be done to implement Security Council Resolution 242. To have a small joint staff working on the problem, even if it was unable to come up with any idea that the two governments adopted, might alter the adversary perception of the situation and thus reduce the danger of superpower involvement even if the Arab-Israeli conflict should again be expressed in open warfare.

As you will see in browsing through the other letters, I intend to publish the collection (with the names of addressees omitted) with the thought that the ideas may be of some interest to a wider audience. If you have any suggestions that might affect the published version, please let me know.

Yours,

ROGER FISHER

Note to the Reader

So far you have been looking over my shoulder at various ideas and suggestions given to people actively and officially concerned with the Arab-Israeli conflict. But officials are not the only ones who make a difference. It is unlikely that you would have read this book unless you, too, had some interest in the Middle East. The Middle East is in a mess. What are you going to do about it?

My suggestion, as you must know, is:

- Identify some individual or organization as your target of influence, somebody who might be able to do what you think ought to be done.
- Formulate just what it is that you would like them to do.
- Communicate with them in a way that makes it more likely that they will do it.

The next few pages are blank, except for your notes and criticisms, your reactions and ideas. A working approach requires work. I have tried to stimulate some thinking and perhaps some action. What happens from here on is up to you.

List of Drafts Included in the Letters

EGYPTIAN

U.N. Resolution 242

United Nations Security Council
Resolution 242 of November 22, 1967

The Security Council,

Expressing its continuing concern with the grave situation in the Middle East,

Emphasizing the inadmissibility of the acquisition of territory by war and the need to work for a just and lasting peace in which every State in the area can live in security,

Emphasizing further that all Member States in their acceptance of the Charter of the United Nations have undertaken a commitment to act in accordance with Article 2 of the Charter,

1. *Affirms* that the fulfillment of Charter principles requires the establishment of a just and lasting peace in the Middle East which should include the application of both the following principles:

(i) Withdrawal of Israeli armed forces from territories occupied in the recent conflict;

(ii) Termination of all claims or states of belligerency and respect for and acknowledgement of the sovereignty, territorial integrity and political independence of every State in the area and their right to live in peace within secure and recognized boundaries free from threats or acts of force;

2. *Affirms further* the necessity

(a) For guaranteeing freedom of navigation through international waterways in the area;

(b) For achieving a just settlement of the refugee problem;

(c) For guaranteeing the territorial inviolability and political independence of every State in the area, through measures including the establishment of demilitarized zones;

3. *Requests* the Secretary-General to designate a Special Representative to proceed to the Middle East to establish and maintain contacts with the States concerned in order to promote agreement and assist efforts to achieve a peaceful and accepted settlement in accordance with the provisions and principles in this resolution;

4. *Requests* the Secretary-General to report to the Security Council on the progress of the efforts of the Special Representative as soon as possible.

Notes

1. *Daedalus,* Summer 1964, pp. 920–41.
2. *Bulletin of Atomic Scientists,* January 1962.
3. *Harvard Law Review,* April 1961, pp. 1130–40.
4. Abdul A. Said, ed., *Theory of International Relations: The Crisis of Relevance* (Englewood Cliffs, N.J.: Prentice Hall, 1968), pp. 43–57.
5. New York: Harper & Row, 1969.
6. London: Allen Lane The Penguin Press, 1971.
7. For the text of Resolution Number 242, adopted by the Security Council on November 22, 1967, see p. 157. Among other provisions, that resolution called upon the Secretary-General to appoint a Special Representative to the Middle East. On November 23, 1967, Secretary-General U Thant invited the Swedish ambassador to Moscow, Dr. Gunnar Jarring, to accept his designation as Special Representative. United Nations, Security Council (Document No. S/8259), 23 November 1967.
8. See *New York Times,* 5 July 1971, p. 4.
9. On June 19, 1970, United States Secretary of State William P. Rogers sent a letter to Egyptian Foreign Minister Mahmoud Riad that incorporated proposals also communicated to Israel and Jordan. In this so-called Rogers Initiative, the Secretary of State proposed that Egypt, Jordan, and Israel designate representatives to discussions to be held under Ambassador Jarring's auspices. He further proposed that the purpose of these discussions be to reach agreement on the establishment of a just and lasting peace based on mutual acknowledgment of each other's sovereignty, territorial integrity, and political independence, and on Israel's withdrawal from occupied territory. Finally,

Rogers proposed a strict ninety-day observance by all parties of the 1967 Security Council cease-fire resolutions (adopted at the time of the Six-Day War).

Egypt accepted the Rogers proposals on July 23, 1970. Despite threats of renewed violence by Palestinian guerrillas, Jordan accepted the proposal on July 26. On August 4 the State Department received Israel's formal acceptance.

10. The resumed cease-fire went into effect on August 7, 1970. The ninety-day cease-fire was extended in November 1970 and again in February 1971. It formally expired on March 7, 1971.

11. In a February 4, 1971, speech to the National Assembly, Egypt's President Sadat offered to permit the immediate clearance of the Suez Canal, blocked since 1967 by ships sunk in the Six-Day War, if Israel would begin a partial withdrawal of its troops from the eastern side of the Canal. Sadat described this proposal as an Egyptian initiative to demonstrate his country's desire for a political settlement with Israel. He did not specify in his speech how far back from the Canal Israeli troops would be expected to withdraw; nor did he mention whether or not Israeli ships would be allowed passage through the Canal. Efforts by the United States to help bring about agreement on such an interim arrangement apparently ended in failure in November 1971.

12. On February 8, 1971, Dr. Jarring delivered identical letters to Israel and Egypt. He requested from Israel a commitment to withdraw to the pre–June 5, 1967, Sinai border in return for satisfactory arrangements regarding demilitarized zones and freedom of navigation through the Suez Canal and the Strait of Tiran. From Egypt Jarring requested a peace agreement with Israel covering the following points: termination of all states' claims of belligerency, acknowledgment of each other's independence and right to secure borders, noninterference in each other's domestic affairs, and cessation of guerrilla attacks against Israel.

13. May 4 through May 6, 1971. See *New York Times,* 5 May, p. 6; 6 May, p. 10; and 7 May, p. 10.

14. Instead of continuing to insist upon the unconditional surrender of Japan, the Potsdam Proclamation of July 26, 1945, referred to "the unconditional surrender of all Japanese armed forces" and promised Japan "freedom of speech, of religion, and of thought," "participation in world trade relations," permission "to maintain such industries as will sustain her economy," "access to . . . raw materials," the withdrawal of occupying forces as soon as certain limited objectives had

been accomplished, and even permission for her surrendering military forces "to return to their homes with the opportunity to lead peaceful and productive lives." *Department of State Bulletin,* 29 July 1945, pp. 137–38.

15. In response to Ambassador Jarring's request of February 8, 1971, that Israel "give a commitment to withdraw its forces from occupied UAR territory to the former international boundary," Israel replied: "Israel will not withdraw to the pre–June 5, 1967, lines." *New Middle East,* April 1971, pp. 44–45.

16. "It does not seem open to any serious question that the United Arab Republic would be authorized to close the Canal. . . ." R. R. Baxter, *The Law of International Waterways* (Cambridge: Harvard University Press, 1964), p. 223.

17. 52 *American Journal of International Law,* January 1958, p. 14.

18. *Newsweek* for December 13, 1971 reports President Anwar Sadat's statement to Arnaud de Borchgrave: ". . . I am ready to meet the Israelis in the Security Council, or with the four powers, in the presence of Ambassador Jarring, to implement the resolution that was designed by the world community to bring permanent peace to the Middle East—and that peace includes Israel, of course."

19. This promise was renewed on December 1, 1971. *New York Times,* 2 December 1971, p. 18.

20. December 1968. See *New York Times,* 9 December, p. 1; 29 December, p. 2.

21. Professor Gottlieb's materials developing concepts for a peaceful settlement in the Middle East currently remain unpublished. A somewhat inaccurate report of his proposal for a "Commonwealth of Palestine" appeared in the *New York Times* on February 23, 1971, p. 2.

Index

About the Author

For more than thirty years the process of coping with conflict has had a continuing interest for Roger Fisher—as a undergraduate major in international law and relations, as a participant in World War II, as a United States government official in Paris during the years of the Marshall Plan, as a Washington lawyer practicing international law, as an adviser to more than one foreign government, as an advocate arguing cases in court, as a consultant on international security affairs to the Department of Defense, and currently as a professor of law at Harvard University, where he specializes in the international field. He is the author of *International Conflict for Beginners* (Harper & Row, 1969), recently published in London under the title *Basic Negotiating Strategy.*

He is a member of the Council on Foreign Relations, the American Society of International Law, and the Commission to Study the Organization of Peace. He is on the board of directors of the Boston World Affairs Council and is a member of the board of trustees of the Hudson Institute.

He was the originator of the national public television series *The Advocates,* which, when he was the program's first executive editor, won television's distinguished Peabody Award for Meritorious Service to Broadcasting.

In connection with *The Advocates'* special broadcasts on the Middle East, Professor Fisher was the last Westerner to have an interview with President Nasser. For the same broadcasts he also met with King Hussein of Jordan and Prime Minister Golda Meir of Israel. In recent months he has made three additional trips to the Middle East.

72 73 74 75 76   10 9 8 7 6 5 4 3 2 1